W. H. Goodfellow

The Industrial Advantages of Lowell, Mass. and Environs

South Lowell, North Chelmsford, South and East Chelmsford, Chelmsford Center,

Dracut, Billerica, North Billerica, Ayer's City, Collinsville and Willow Dale

W. H. Goodfellow

The Industrial Advantages of Lowell, Mass. and Environs
South Lowell, North Chelmsford, South and East Chelmsford, Chelmsford Center, Dracut, Billerica, North Billerica, Ayer's City, Collinsville and Willow Dale

ISBN/EAN: 9783337180591

Printed in Europe, USA, Canada, Australia, Japan

INDUSTRIAL ADVANTAGES

OF

LOWELL, MASS.

AND ENVIRONS.

South Lowell, North Chelmsford, South and East Chelmsford, Chelmsford Center, Dracut, Billerica, North Billerica, Ayer's City, Collinsville, and Willow Dale.

COMPILED UNDER THE MANAGEMENT OF

W. H. GOODFELLOW, SR.,

AND THE REPRESENTATIVE CITIZENS OF LOWELL.

ALSO

A SERIES OF COMPREHENSIVE SKETCHES OF THEIR

REPRESENTATIVE MANUFACTURING AND COMMERCIAL ENTERPRISES.

LOWELL, MASS.:
W. H. GOODFELLOW, PUBLISHER,
1895.

THE PAPER

ON WHICH THIS BOOK IS PRINTED WAS MADE EXPRESSLY FOR IT BY

THE HUDSON VALLEY PAPER CO.,

520 and 522 Broadway, Albany, N. Y.

THE PHOTOGRAPHS

WERE MADE BY

WESCOTT AND COGGESHALL & PIPER.

THE ILLUSTRATIONS

WERE ENGRAVED BY

COGGESHALL & PIPER,

Central Street, Lowell, Mass.

THE

INDUSTRIAL ADVANTAGES

OF

LOWELL, MASS.

AT THE outset of this volume it is better in lieu of all professions to state that it in no way professes to be a history of Lowell, but on the contrary is devoted to an account of the present condition and development of the chief industrial and commercial enterprises located here, and to the advantages and attractions the city and vicinity have to offer those looking for a favorable location for the establishment of new enterprises. Arguing that no single fact can be more convincing as to the superior advantages of Lowell as a site of industrial operation, than the success and prosperity of this enterprise already in operation here.

Much space has been given over to descriptive sketches of the leading manufacturing and commercial houses of this community, and as many of these have grown from small beginnings to be the largest of the kind in the world, for new beginners may confidently expect the like results under able progressive management. No city in America affords a more prolific theme for favorable comment than Lowell. It is one of the most flourishing cities on the American continent, and equally thriving. It has enjoyed a world wide prominence for over a century, and yet its growth has been solid and substantial, rather than too rapid, and it ranks today with an urban population of about 92,000, and a suburban corporation of over 55,000 whose interests are practically coincident with Lowell. It is the third city both in population and amount of business transacted, and in value of products turned out from its manufactures. The beautiful, progressive and flourishing city of Lowell will soon celebrate the One Hundredth anniversary of its foundation.

The history of Lowell is said to have begun in the year of 1822. It is favorably located on the notable Merrimack and Concord Rivers. The Merrimack dividing Lowell almost in the center giving the main street, which is Merrimack, the term of East Merrimack Street. The city is compactly built upon a somewhat elevated plain, beginning from the Merrimack River extending back to a range of hills terminating abruptly about two miles and a half east.

These hills rise to an altitude of about three to four hundred feet, and their slopes are dotted with Public Institutions of commanding proportions and handsome mansions, they offer charming views of the unchanging surrounding vales, dells, meandering rivers, fringed beyond by sky kissing upheavals of nature. The trees standing on the outskirts of the busy growing city, stand like sentinels keeping watch and ward over factories filled with whirling wheels of machinery which offer numerous and active markets of commerce, receiving from and shipping to every part of the globe the products of the knitting mills, soil and mechanism of skilled craftsmen in all the branches of industrial enterprises. Even the very hill tops are capped by palatial residences, busy factories, sanctuaries with Heaven pointing spires, the streets are lined with toiling members of the community, and stores packed with commodities essential to the substance and enjoyment of life.

The city is built mostly south of the Pawtucket Falls, and extending along the banks and canals of the Merrimack and Concord Rivers for a distance of about four miles. The former river just below Pawtucket Falls forms a curve which evidently some time back flowed southward, but changed its course and empties into the Atlantic at Newburyport.

The principal business thoroughfare lies between two branches of the Merrimack River, and both branches unite with the Concord at right angles at the termination of the main business street. With the exception of this one street, the city is regularly laid out, intersecting each other in various places at right angles. They are generally sixty feet wide, though several have a width of eighty feet. They are well paved and cleanly kept. There are a few shade trees in the business vicinity and they are especially thick in the residential section of the city, some of them varying in height from fifty to one hundred feet. From the hilly slopes on the eastern side of the city to the Merrimack River, and with an intersecting system of well built sewers, the drainage is about as perfect as can possibly be desired by any community fully alive to the responsible necessity, guarding the health of the people by the adoption of the best sanitary regulations that modern science can suggest.

Lowell is surrounded by many populous and thriving towns possesing great manufacturing and mercantile enterprises, that contribute materially to her growth and prosperity. Chief among these essentials oft shoots of the city are South Lowell, on the north side of the Concord River, and on the opposite side of the Concord River is the busy village of Billerica. At a radius of three or four miles from that place lies North Chelmsford. East and South Chelmsford and Chelmsford Centre, with their busy factories and work shops which are yearly increasing their industrial establishments.

Ayer's City, also one of the nearest suburbs, is distinguished by having within its limits situated on Hale's Brook, by which it derives its power, is a number of thriving manufacturing concerns. This notable suburb derived its name from the well known Ayer family, who in years gone by were in possession of the surrounding property.

Pawtucketville, lies on the Northwestern bank of the Merrimack River, along which it has one of the most beautiful boulevards, being over three hundred feet wide with double giant walks, gardens and foot paths. It has a driven well to supply the roadway with sufficient sprinkling operation during the hot months of the summer, and keeps the earth's clothing in a fresh state of condition.

Lowell itself has within the past few years displayed in every department of commerce and manufactures an unusual amount of activity and enterprise, notwithstanding the financial depressions of the past few years. Lowell has more than held its own according to statistics. New buildings of every description for residences, works and commercial emporiums have been reared on every hand and sound progressive business management prevails over the whole community. This, coupled with the fact that Lowell occupies all exceptional advantages and location in respect of care, natural facilities for the economical conduct of its great and varied manufacturing enterprises, and that it possesses ample transportation facilities by rail to every part of the continent, accounts for the evidence of thrift and prosperity to be found on every hand. The situation is such that Lowell commands far reaching and invaluable system ot transportation that secures rates as a most favorable character for transportation in any direction.

WILILIAM F. COURTNEY.

Biographical Sketch of Lowell's Present Mayor.

His achievement as a lawyer, as a member of the Legislature and City Solicitor, a companion of labor and a man of conservative learnings. William F. Courtney, present Democratic Mayor of Lowell, was 39 years old the 10th of last December. He was born in Belvidere, December 10, 1855, but during most of his life he has resided in Centralville with his parents. Mr. Courtney is unmarried, but he does not keep a bachelors'

hall in the ordinary acception of the term. To say that Mr. Courtney is a gentlemanby instinct and breeding, is to say what everybody who knows him will say; he is a man of honor in all his business and professional relations, as his fellow members of the bar can testify. He is the soul of honesty, and the personification of integrity. He is a man whom his friends love and admire, respect, esteem, and it is due in no small degree to the careful training he received from his mother, who is one of the most intelligent and estimable kind of women.

Mr. Courtney as a lawyer received his early education in the Public Schools of Lowell. He studied law in the office of Charles F. Donnelly, Esq., of Boston, at the time when Hon. Owen A. Galvin was a student there; attended the Harvard Law School and finished his course in 1879; formed a partnership with James J. McCaffery, now a judge in St. Paul, Minn.; was later a partner of Isaac S. Morse, who was District Attorney for 17 years with offices in the Rogers' building, Boston.

For several years past Mr. Courtney has had his office in the Mansur Block in this city. He has built up an extensive and profitable practice, and is regarded as one of the foremost members of the Middlesex Bar. Mr. Courtney has been counsel in many important cases. Most of the points which he has raised have been decided in his favor by the Supreme Court. It is said that Mr. Courtney's name is quoted in the Court Reports in connection with points of law, decided in his favor, more frequently than that of any other lawyer of his age and extent of practice.

A notable case was that of the Commonwealth vs. Howe. This was a case of the alleged ballot box stuffing on the license question in Ward 2, Lowell. Howe was convicted in the lower Court, but Mr. Courtney carried the case to the Supreme Court on the ground that there was no law to punish the offense alleged and the court sustained the point. As a result of this decision, Governor Ames sent a special message to the General Court pointing out the loop-hole in the law, and recommending remedial legislature, and in 1887 the present law covering such cases was enacted.

MR. COURTNEY AS CITY SOLICITOR.

In 1887 Mr. Courtney was elected City Solicitor and served in that office for one year as counsel for the city, during which time he was engaged in many important cases, with which he was equally successful in the courts. The Hon. James C. Abbott, who was Mayor at that time, said that Mr. Courtney was the best solicitor the city ever had.

Mr. Courtney is greatly in favor of booming the industrial advantages of our city, and that although the instigator of this book is a young man, he feels that it is worthy of acceptance to the manufacturing and commercial industries of the city of Lowell.

Memorial Building.

Manufacturers

The right place to successfully manufacture is evidently at a point where the raw material accumulates only, and where at the same time there is cheap power and advanced and ample facilities for marketing the products. Lowell has, for many years, furnished these combinations by railroad systems connecting the city with the market of the South, East, West and North, being inland less than thirty (30) miles. Navigation upon the Atlantic Ocean has been a great help to this city. Material necessarily accumulates within each surrounding region. Canadian forests for lumber is easily reached by rail in a very short time. Trades can be established here by manufacturers superior to those of larger cities, for the reason that while greater facilities are found here, at the same time the best and most central position are available at comparatively little cost, and numerous sites on the line of railroad, Merrimack and Concord River banks are open for use.

Iron, lumber and other materials used for manufacturing purposes can be brought to Lowell better than to many competing centers as we have better facilities for distributing the products. The manufacturer who locates here will find everything at hand for the successful furtherance of his enterprises and a friendly and helping hand will be offered him by every citizen of the community; in brief, some of the first advantages and attractions of Lowell, Mass., are:

First, its location in a most fertile and attractive portion of the United States, and in one of the most thriving and prosperous counties in the state.

Second, it possesses the advantages of railroad and railway transportation in all directions. and all competing lines express and show a liberal spirit toward all manufacturing enterprises.

Third, it is so situated as to use the vast amount of waters for manufacturing purposes of the Merrimack and Concord Rivers, Hale's Brook, Beaver Brook and Black Brook, all of which give power to the suburban manufacturing enterprises as well as that of Lowell.

Fourth, it has direct railroad connection with the vast coal regions of Nova Scotia and North Pennsylvania.

Fifth, it has direct railroad connections with the industries of northern countries.

Sixth, the water supply is adequate for all purposes of manufacturing facilities, and has a special system of driven wells for domestic supply.

Seventh, statistics show that it is one of the healthiest cities in the Union.

Eighth, its public school system affords excellent educating advantages and facilities.

Ninth, the cost of living here is much less than in any large city in the state or in the country.

No city in the Union offers such advantages to the small and larger manufacturers as does Lowell at the present time. The conducting of new enterprises will increase the trades for the retail merchants to establish successful mercantile operations.

The question has frequently been asked, What can be manufactured in Lowell? The simplest answer and absolutely true one is, *everything*. A good idea of what can be done may be obtained by a glance at the

Pawtucket Walk.

impression of buying for less money) has almost vanished from public opinion as people have learned by experience that Lowell merchants compete in every respect with the large houses of Boston. The wholesale and retail commerce of this city covers a large extent of territory, which is thickly settled with wealth and is conducted with sufficient enterprise and success.

The manufacturing concerns of Lowell have made great extraditions for the trade in every part of the world, and the smaller concerns of the city have succeeded in placing their goods to the trade of North-Western New York, Vermont, Massachusetts, Rhode Island, Connecticut and Maine, and keeping their portion of the trades mentioned. To be sure the important metropolis of Boston is located less than 30 miles from Lowell, connected both by steam and electric cars, the electric cars running through the cities of Lawrence and Haverhill on their way to Boston,

Coal Supply.

Among the conditions which have for many years united in promoting the growth of the city is the cheapness of fuel for domestic purposes and for the supply of the manufacturing industries., No city in the state without any exception has better connections with the coal deposits for obtaining its fuel than has been proven to Lowell commissioners The difference during the last 20 years has ranged from 10 to 30 per cent as a comparison of sales in the various towns will show, that the cost of living and the cost of production is largely graded on the price of fuel. The fact here stated is one that may be taken into consideration in estimating the advantages of our city and towns as a place of residence and especially as a location for manufacturing purposes.

The extent of the business conducted by the large coal dealers engaged for instance, in Lowell, without roads, the figures exhibit the most astonishing proportions. The direct railroad connection with the Atlantic Ocean, water connections with the coal fields of Pennsylvania and Nova Scotia, and the competition existing here between rival corporations, which are extensively numerous, and shippers of this valuable product in relation to fixing the delivering price of coal in Lowell, places coal at lower figures than are enjoyed in other important manufacturing centers in the state.

The Press.

Ten daily papers are published in Lowell. Two of the dailies also publish weeklies. There are two daily French papers, one semi-weekly and two monthlies.

Prospects of the Future.

The location of Lowell is one which renders it impossible for any combination of circumstances to arrest its growth, either as a place of industrial business advantages or residential seats The past of Lowell having furnished a record of continuous and sustained growth, it is a fair presumption that tne future will present results of extraordinary advance or even excel expectations. This is a time of great industry and the classes of the nineteenth century are rapidly surrounding us with such evidences

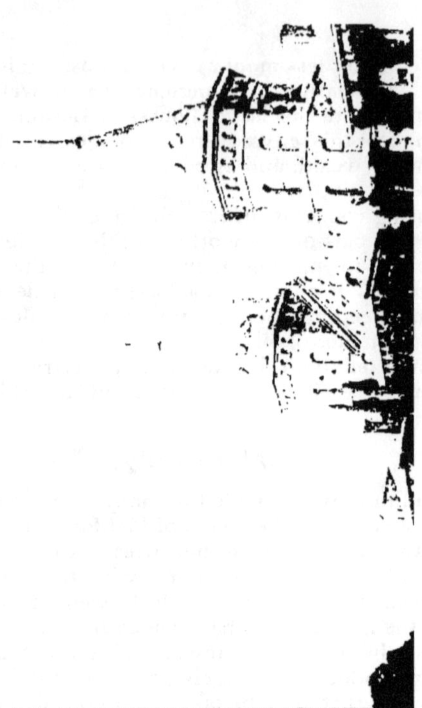

Lowell Jail.

of their amazing powers in their results of steam and electricity. Already the development of electrical science have given us a revelation in the method of obtaining motive powers which bids fair to supplant all others. In the utilization of all the resources which nature has furnished or science unveiled, there is every reason to believe that Lowell will be fully abreast with the most progressive cities in the Union.

It has no lack of men with business activity equal to the improvement of every trade, and it is safe to predict that the historians of industry of the future will be able to point back to those of to-day, as we now point back to the beginning of a greater and better destiny.

Granite.

The suburbs of Lowell have many granite quarries which produce and place upon the market some of the most valuable building material. They are located on the line which divides Massachusetts from New Hampshire in places called Graniteville, Acton and many other localities which are numerous in that location. The largest works located at West Chelmsford are owned by H. E. Fletcher, which are supposed to be the finest in that vicinity.

Water Works.

The subject of first importance in any city is the character and quality of its public water supply. Lowell is in possession of a water supply drawn from driven wells, which are located many feet above the level of either river on both sides. Its distribution contains three systems of service, high, medium and low pressure, covering different parts of the city. The storage or reservoir capacity of the wells in one combination are said to cover the capacity of about four hundred million gallons. There are about 55 miles of pipe in use and when the present system is completely finished, Lowell will have a gravity system only furnishing pure spring water.

Cars and Bridges.

The electric cars convey patrons to all the surrounding villages which are numerous, to four summer resorts and to the cities of Lawrence, Haverhill and Boston. The Lowell & Suburban Street Railway Co. is now constructing a road connecting the city of Nashua, N. H., with the city of Lowell by the way of a summer resort. It can be said that no city within our limited distance has better accommodations than Lowell, there being two lines running to Boston, the B. & M. R. R. Western Division and the B. & M. R. R. Southern Division, so that a train can be had at almost any hour during the day and evening.

Bridges are numerous in Lowell, it having about seven railroad and four foot bridges, the principal ones connecting the main street to Centralville, Pawtucketville, Belvidere. All of the main bridges are of iron construction.

The Streets.

Almost the first subject of remark of visitors to the city, and one worthy so both on account of their width, cleanliness and industrial appearance with which they are almost universally lined with working people at 6.15

St. Anne's Church.

o'clock in the morning, at noon and from 6 o'clock until half-past 10 p. m., especially evenings that the retail merchants keep open, such evenings being Monday, Friday and Saturday.

The streets of Lowell are regularly and tastefully laid out, with the exception of the manufacturing portion of the city, which is more or less cut up in that district for the large manufacturing buildings. Merrimack street, the main thoroughfare, is wide and spacious. Central is next in importance, followed by Prescott, Palmer, Middlesex, Dutton, Shattuck and Gorham. There are innumerable residential sections which are beautiful and possess commanding views. The main streets of the city are well paved with granite.

Police.

The city has an efficient police force, furnishing ample protection for the citizens. Most of them are large, portly men. The force consists of about 113 men, under the supervision of a superintendent, who is assisted by a deputy superintendent, one night captain, three lieutenants, two sergeants, two inspectors, two liquor inspectors, two warrant officers, two keepers, one matron. There are three reliefs, going on duty at 8 a. m., 6 p. m. and 12 p. m. respectively. The are five mounted police detailed for Centralville, Pawtucketville, Ward Four, Ayer's City and Belvidere. Great credit is due to Mr. Michael Burns, the electrician who with two assistants is kept busy on repairs of the fifty seven boxes. The Gamewell system is in use, and it has been proven that no other city in the New England states has as much business or is better equipped than the efficient police force of Lowell.

There is only one station, and that is in the same building with the municipal court, over which Judge Hadley presides assisted by two clerks.

The Fire Department

Consists of a well trained brigade, and being thoroughly efficient, indeed reflects the greatest credit on the city. It is under the control of a committee of the city government. The city is covered with fire alarm boxes, there being 227, at convenient points, telegraph system, 7 engine companies, 7 hose and one hook and ladder company.

Climate and Sanitary Conditions.

No condition is more essential to the continued prosperity and happiness of the community than health. Statistics prove that this city is one of the most healthful cities in the country. Its climate is pure and genial, the temperature is modified by three sources of two rivers. The city is subject to no prevailing disease, is well drained, and its sanitary condition is well regulated by an efficient Board of Health. In comparison with other cities the percentage of mortality in combination with the vast amount of working people, Lowell has about the lowest in the state. The natural features of soil, climate and topography is unable to describe more accurately the advantages which this location has to offer. The practical well built sewers pervert to make perfect the sanitary system. Typhoid fever, one of the direst enemies of large cities, is in one sense practically unknown here in proportion to the several cities in the state.

Merrimack Street.

Societies.

Lowell has numerous organizations for fraternal, beneficial and helpful purposes, all of which are in a flourishing condition and are accomplishing the object of their existence.

Educational.

Lowell in educational institutions is the peer to any city of its size in the community, and the character of schools and colleges in her corporation limits shows exclusively that this is the seat of true learning of the many attractions offered, which excel those of vast cities, to acquire the conditions desired in connection with industrial advantages. Here the man with or without fortune can alike secure the boon of solid education for his children, to be followed up when desired with extensive and elegant culture. Advantages are offered by public and private institutions as the case requires. Too much can hardly be written in regard to our public school system in extent, and the prominence which it occupies, offering all branches of education to the pupils from the primary to the higher grades of the high school without any cost of tuition. This admirable organization, beginning with numerous kindergarten departments, embraces every grade of scholarship up to the free high school. There are over 51 public schools in Lowell, and about 7 parochial schools, 1 business college, 1 academy, 1 reform school besides numerous kindergartens.

Churches.

The churches of Lowell are widely distributed over the city, and are confined to no one section. The ecclesiastical edifices are mostly of substantial and enduring proportions, and the condition of their financial affairs attest the most skilful and conservative direction.

The number of church societies of all denominations holding regular services, either in their own edifices or other suitable places, is about 50.

The Public Institutions.

The public institutions of Lowell are of great importance and usefulness, presenting very substantial evidence of the city's accummulating wealth, and of its eminently thorough and practical character. Among them is the beautiful City Hall, built at immense cost, a picture of which is found on the frontispiece.

The most elegant Public Library which excels any in the state and one that its citizens should feel proud of. The new Postoffice which has recently been dedicated, is of much interest, it being made completely of granite, containing all the latest improvements in the assortment and distribution of mail.

The Young Men's Christian Association, not having the finest building by any means at present, intends to erect one in the near future.

The Reform School occupies a prominent place, and the Jail and Infirmary are placed among the features for good work in elevating the tone of society.

The Old Ladies' Home, the Ayer Home for young ladies and children, the Edson Orphanage, the Catholic Female Aslyum, and hospitals

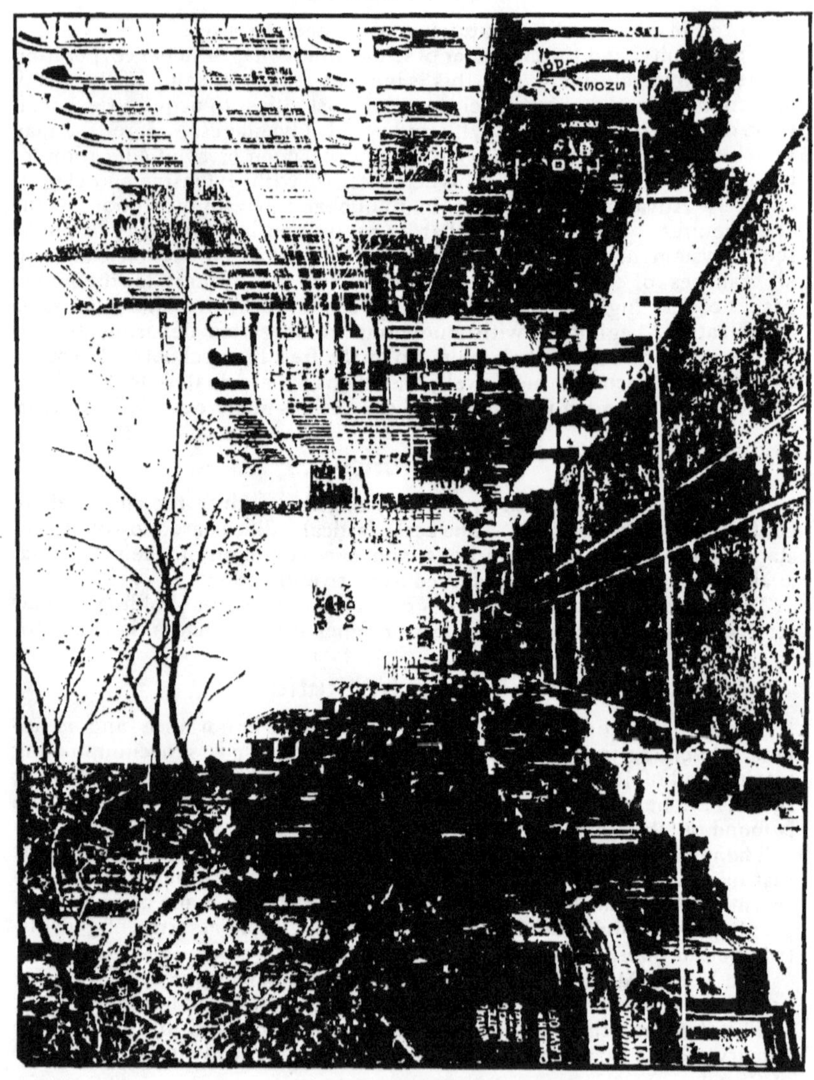

Central Street.

among which are the St. John's, the City Hospital and the Lowell General Hospital.

Amusements.

Lowell being so readily accessible to the metropolis enjoys the luxury of first-class theatrical entertainments by the best theatrical companies who visit this city, and are always sure of a generous support. There are two well supported and managed theatres maintained, one being magnificent, called the Lowell Opera House. We have second and third class and a fourth which is hardly worth mentioning; they are called Huntington Hall, Music Hall and the Bijou. The first two have a very large seating capacity. A summer resort which patrons are conveyed to by electric cars, called Lakeview, which is romantic and historic in its surroundings. It has a dance hall, theatre, bowling alleys, pavilion, band stand, and in fact everything of interest to the pleasure seeking public. There is a place close by it even more romantic in its surroundings called Willow Dale, which is accessible by carriage and steamboat. Mountain Rock is directly opposite Willow Dale, which is said to be the coming interest of that section. In the summer time there is at least one hundred pleasure and row boats upon its lake with two pleasure steamers plying upon its surface at all times.

The present Lowell is magnificent and full of promise. It is the busiest and most progressive city in the community of equal extent and capacity standing between the two great oceans. Its natural advantages were never better supplemented by its acquired resources for the development of its progress than they are to-day, and we are able to obtain homes, prosperity and happiness alike waiting for us on every hand. Lowell is the home of the intelligent, vigorous, refined and wealthy, with a past full of interest and a present full of earnestness and a future full of brightness.

Lowell presents a thousand attractions to the student, the tourist, the statesman, the wage earner, and greatest of all to that most direct of all, to the localists, the enterprising capitalist seeking safe investments in real estate, or the establishment of attractive industries.

The time is not far distant when the one hundred and fifty thousand residents of Lowell and environs will have become double in number, and will be second to none of the manufacturing industrial cities in the United States, as well as that of the New England states of the most attractive city for the display of all commercial enterprises.

Bird's Eye View of Lowell, Mass

LOWELL, MASS.

Some of the Leading Industries and Principal Mercantile Establishments, with Sketches of their Foundation, Progress and History, and Notes on Character and Extent of their Operations.

PUTNAM & SON,

Clothiers, Central St.

Among the retail enterprises that well illustrate the perfection attained in all departments of retail clothing houses and gents' furnishing establishments established in Lowell, a prominent and influential one is that of Putnam & Sons, which occupies a most important location at the corner of Central and Warren sts. Messrs. Putnam & Son's enterprise was originally founded in 1846 by Addison Putnam. His son, F. P. Putnam, became associated in the business later.

There is no clothing store, or probably no other concern outside of the metropolis, who are more favorably known and whose goods are in more universal use than those of Messrs. Putnam & Sons' establishment, for they handle only goods of high class, hand made garments, which assures the close inspection of the most conservative buyers, in fact the place is called "to order ready made place" for public sentiment goes to show that they feel as well satisfied with goods bought at Putnam's as they do of a tailor made suit.

The firm has a most elegant displaying corner with a floorage of about 100 x 150 square feet, which enables them to carry an immense stock of their representative lines. Messrs. Putnam & Sons furnish employment for about twelve steady clerks, twelve extras and a half dozen boys. The high reputation attained by this house in the past has been fully maintained under their management of personal attention, which goes to show

Ayer Home for Women.

ample capacity of conservative business progression, and the business has steadily increased ever since its birth.

H. B. ROBINSON,

Central St.

There is always special interest attached to a confectionery establishment and particular attention is called to that of H. B. Robinson, whose place of business No. 9 Central street, is a most prominent confectionery establishment in the city of Lowell. Mr. Robinson has a thorough knowledge of confectionery as well as large practical business experience. This establishment is surely a factor in the city of Lowell, Mr. Robinson not only having business interests at the above place, but scattered interests in a number of other places. Combined in a marked degree the house of H. B. Robinson of this city is a representative house of its kind. He is also author of many fancy goods in his line, and is widely accepted as an expert in candy making.

Mr. Robinson holds some of the finest trade in the city of Lowell and under his personal supervision the business is increasing very rapidly.

Mr. Robinson is not only a progressive business man, but holds a high esteem in commercial circles for liberal and fair methods, which justly entitles him to the prominent success achieved in his chosen field of endeavor.

E. D. STEELE & Co.,

Clothiers and Furnishers, Corner Central and Prescott Sts.

Although E. D. Steele & Co. have been in Lowell less than three years, they have established themselves among the leading concerns of the city. That they are popular with the people cannot be disputed as they have more than doubled the business since the store came under their management. Their store is centrally located, well appointed and thoroughly equipped with all modern conveniences for handling their large business with facility and promptness.

Steele & Co. have two other prosperous clothing establishments, one at Pepperell, Mass., and one at St. Johnsbury, Vermont. The St. Johnsbury store has been for years one of the best in northern Vermont, and it is a well established fact that there is no clothing house that gives better satisfaction than theirs. The great bulk of their clothing is from the thoroughly reliable house of Davis, Hopkiers & Co. This firm is conceded by all experienced dealers to be the equal of any house in the business. All their goods are union made and bear the union label.

P. DAVEY,

Furniture and Undertaking, Market St.

This prominent and important house has grown from small beginnings to be a leading factor in the supply of furniture and undertaking materi als. Mr. Davey's business was established in 1887 in the undertaking department and a year later in 1888 he added thereby to the furniture business, which has steadily increased daily and has developed with the growth of Lowell, and is today one of the leading furniture and undertaking establishments of the city.

The premises occupied consist of a large commodious four story brick building, facing Market street, at No. 134, opposite Palmer street, having a frontage of about 40 feet and 100 feet deep, with a side entrance where goods are received and shipped. The upper story has storage rooms where is displayed, in connection with his first floor, furniture of every description. Mr. Davey was overseer of the poor under Mayor Donovan's administration. He has been a resident and merchant for nineteen years. He is about 50 years of age, and is an energetic, efficient business man.

His large business has only been attained by progressive, enterprising, straightforward dealings, which can be vouched for by the general public, and the progressive business management has, of course, a great deal to do with it.

A. GOVOSTES,

Confectionery and Candy Manufacturer, 234 Merrimack St.

One of the most popular and attractive confectionery stores in the city is that of A. Govostes which is located in the old City Hall building at 234 Merrimack street, which has been remodelled, refitted and is now one of the most attractive stores of its kind in the city of Lowell. The interior of the place is fitted up with plate mirrors, with lattice work dividing the ice cream parlors from that of the confectionery salesroom, the rear portion being solely disconnected from that of the order department. Every pound of candy is reliable both in material and workmanship, all of which is strictly hand made, the product of skilled hands of wide experience. The facilities of the house for catering are not surpassed by any house in the city, as the long experience of Mr. Govostes has a wide reputation in Boston, Mass., and Manchester, N. H. Each store is conducted under the most modern business methods, and goods obtained from this house can be relied upon as prices are in keeping with the quality.

A cordial invitation is given to the lovers of first-class confectionery, ice cream and soda of all flavors, to call and inspect the delicious articles manufactured for candy judges. Although the Lowell establishment has been running but a short time the business is increasing and it is safe to predict that the advantages under which the inducements are offered to the public and the economical distribution of goods warrants sure success to this finely appointed house.

BREAD OF LIFE.

In the new Odd Fellows' building situated on Branch street just above the junction of Middlesex, is the old historic building of the Odd Fellows' hall, in which is located what is known as the Highland Bakery. Although Mr. F. E. Desautels has been there hardly a year, yet he is making a slow but sure headway in the success of domestic and fancy bakeries. The line which his business embraces is home made, milk and American breads, fresh every day; hot rolls, biscuits, buns, pastry, fancy pies always in stock, and he is turning his attention to catering for parties and festivals. Ice creams he delivers to any part of the city, at both whole-sale and retail. The number of his location is 129 Branch street. He has a branch store at the corner of Bridge street. He has been in business no less than 14 years. It is well to say that the people of the Highlands consider him worthy of their patronage, he being accommodating, pleasing in address and exceedingly prompt in the delivery of special orders.

J. L. CHALIFOUX.

Chapter from the History of a Representative Lowell Merchant, the Acknowledged Leader in His Line.

A true and well known writer has said: "Few men come to greatness, most drift on with the current having no special plan or aim. They lived where their fathers lived, taking no thought beyond their neighborhood and city and die in their little line of social life." As these words are all too true it is only right and proper that the story of the successful men should be told, and told in such a manner as to awaken ambition and stir the spirit of all mankind. Among the men of our time whose success in business affairs justly entitles him to particular mention, is Mr. J. L. Chalifoux of this city. He is one of the representative merchants of today, shrewd, alert, enterprising and progressive, honorable in all his transactions and thoroughly judicious in his movements. He has built up a colossal interest, and Lowell is proud to honor him among her worthy and most highly respected citizens. As his name would indicate Mr. Chalifoux is of French birth. He came to Lowell in 1863 beginning life in a very small way. For seven years he was employed as a clerk in a clothing store, working on a salary of five dollars a week. In 1875, having succeeded through strict economy in saving a considerable amount of money, he started in business for himself, opening a small store and conducting operations on a strictly cash basis. His first bale of goods to order he paid for in ten days time, and

Lowell Opera House.

he has pursued the same policy from that day to this, paying cash and selling for cash. His discriminating taste combined with the knowledge he had gained as to the best sources of supply, enabled him to furnish goods of the most attractive character for the selection of his customers.

Small interests grew to larger ones, and business steadily expanded requiring increase of facilities necessary from time to time. He remained in the first store four years. At the expiration of that time he removed to larger quarters. He was at the second stand four years more, going to still more commodious quarters. At the end of another four years he made still another change, taking possession of his present elegant premises, in the finest business block in the city, called the Central Block, at the junction of Central and Middle streets. At this location Mr. Chalifoux has the largest clothing store in the state of Massachusetts outside of Boston. He occupies the ground floor of the immense building, commanding a floor space of twenty thousand square feet. He carries a magnificent stock of artistic ready-made clothing for men, boys and children, a hat department, splendid shoe department, and he has just added a ladies' waist department.

Extensive as are the interests involved in the business of this establishment Mr. Chalifoux is ambitious, and his talents are comprehensive enough to reach out to a far distant field. He maintains and has done so since the year of 1890, a branch of his business at Birmingham, Ala. Here he follows the same policy pursued in his New England field, that is the production of business on a cash basis. This way of doing business is new in the South, and has created a great commotion in business circles. His success was undoubted from the beginning, therefore, many other business men have been led to adopt his system.

Mr. Chalifoux is very popular wherever he is known. He holds a number of positions of trust and of public responsibility, and his opinion in regard to financial and business matters are greatly sought after and highly respected. He is ex-president of the Lowell Board of Trade, honorable member of the board of directors of the Old Lowell National Bank, and a trustee of the Lowell General Hospital. He is well known throughout this section as a self-made man. He has come to the high position he holds among men by energy, integrity and determination to win. His career is well worthy the study of those who aim to achieve business success.

LOWELL TRUNK AND HARNESS MANUFACTORY,

No. 23 and 27 Middle St.

George F. Allen is the proprietor of an enterprise that contributes not a little in the development of the industrial resources of Lowell, and we are safe in saying he is the leading one of his kind in the city.

Mr. Allen is 56 years of age, and was established in business in the year of 1866. He has been located in one spot for over 18 years. He was born in the state of Vermont. His father conducted the same line of business for many years before him. His line embraces the following goods:

Horse clothing, such as harnesses, whips, blankets and harness trimmings. He gives special attention to fine harnesses to order. A specialty of his business is trunks, bags, valises, pocket-books, music cases and small articles of every description.

He is generally well known to the community of Lowell as a whole souled, upright business man. All of his goods are offered to the trade at prices as low as is consistent with the quality.

UNION BRASS AND COMPOSITION FOUNDRY,

Corner of Dutton and Hayden Sts.

A leading and important factor of the brass industry of this city is the well known establishment of the Union Brass Foundry, proprietors of which are John and Patrick H. Ryan, who for many years have exclusively devoted their time in the distribution of brass castings to the thickly settled population of Lowell.

This house was originally founded in 1889, and has since been under the control of its present proprietors. They have a two story wooden structure and run four furnaces. They also have a ware house of large proportions which is occupied by waste material of junk which affords a storage accommodation for many hundred pounds of baled material. The rest of the premises are all utilized for the manufacture of brass castings.

Mr. Ryan is an expert brass and composition broker, and an authority on the subject. He gives his personal attention to the purchase and sale of all stock, and carefully superintends the overlooking of the entire foundry. Consumers of brass castings will find this house a reliabie and fair dealing one with which to enter into pleasant and profitable business relations. Mr. Ryan is a progressive business man and ambitious to afford the greatest facilities to the trade. The success and prominence he has attained in this field of industry are alike creditable to his honorable business methods and to the commercial resources of Lowell.

HARNESS AND HORSE CLOTHING EMPORIUM,

494 Middlesex St.

In the year of 1860 S. L. Butman began to do business at number 494 Middlesex street, in the line of harness making and horse clothing of every description. In 1891 Mr. S. L. Butman died and left the business in the charge of his surviving family. A. L. Butman, his son, now conducts the business. He is about 28 years of age, energetic, wide awake, eager, active and is a steady, upright business man. Any man having dealings with him will find him upright. For workmanship on heavy and light harnesses he is first-class. There can be found at this establishment feed bags, whips, blankets, shaft supporters, fly nets, ear nets and halters. You will also find all attachments and sections of the line at the very lowest possible prices. Call and see him when you want a special boot made for your horse. He is excellent on such work and makes a specialty of harness repairing.

LOWELL SCALE WORKS.

Manufacturers of Platform and Counter Scales, Fletcher St.

The importance of using absolutely correct scales for weighing commodities can hardly be estimated, both buyer and seller being equally interested, the former in obtaining all that he pays for, the latter in maintaining his reputation for fair and honest dealing. Great mechanical skill and long experience are requisite to success of the manufacturing of an appliance upon which so much depends, and for that reason a purchaser of scales should make sure that the devices offered him are the products of a well and old established concern of known standing, or at least of scale experts.

The works on Fletcher street comprise a substantial and commodious three story brick front building, 40 feet front and 120 feet deep, fitted up with a comprehensive plan of machinery and appliances, including a 10-horse power electric motor of approved style. A considerable number of mechanics are employed, some of whom have been there for many years,

The output comprises a variety of counter and platform scales. The "New England Union," single and double-beam scoop, scale capacity half an ounce to two hundred and forty pounds. The "Lowell" counter scale, capacity half an ounce to twenty-five pounds, and an "Even Balance," capacity of four pound and eight pound, with and without side beam. Every scale is fully guarranteed and they are thoroughly reliable, while the prices are remarkably low.

This industry is growing rapidly in the city of Lowell. These scales are made to conform to all foreign standards and are in use all over the United States, and are being exported largely to the West Indies, Mexico, Central and South America, Australia, and other countries. The works operated to their full capacity can turn out six thousand scales of all classes annually.

HARVEY HADLEY.

Meats, Vegetables, Oysters and Provisions.

This enterprise is one of the oldest and most important in its line in the section of the Highlands. It has been prominently before the trade for the past 15 years. It was established in 1880 by its present owner, Mr. Harvey Hadley. This business has never had a change of hands since its birth to the present day. The quarters of the house embrace a large and commodious store which affords ample accommodations for the large stock which he carries, and also for the prompt fulfilment of orders and a trade has been developed that extends generally throughout every district of Lowell. The firm are receivers of foreign and domestic fruits in all seasons of the year. They make a leading specialty in oysters during Fall, Winter and Spring months.

Mr. Hadley is 60 years of age and is closely identified with the commercial progress of Lowell and fully alive to the maintenance of the honorable record of their house, which has been enjoyed by him for over 15 years.

Lowell City Hall.

CHEEVER & RUSSELL,

Retail Grocers and Provision Merchants.

The leading and prominent representative of the retail grocery, flour product and provision trade, Messrs. Cheever & Russell, was originally established in the year of 1883 in a small way at number 17 Branch street. Never having a change in the concern, it is annually increasing its trade, and developing a trade throughout the city of Lowell in an astonishing way. They are in touch with Vermont butter makers, and it is said that their butter is superior to many brands sold in Lowell. The premises occupied by them at present is a large and spacious place, having two large show windows, a fine floor space which is replete with a large and complete stock of staple and fancy groceries, teas, syrups, molasses, flour, which are offered to the trade at the lowest prices.

The individual members of the firm are Messrs. D. K. Cheever and H. H. Russell. Both are enterprising and progressive merchants, thoroughly conversant with all the requirements of the trade in this market, they give their close personal attention to all the details of the business in the interest of their customers.

GEORGE H. BATCHELDER & CO.,

Bicycle Dealers, Branch St.

The site now occupied by the well-known bicycle dealers of the firm of G. H. Batchelder & Co. is located at No. 87 Branch street. Mr. G. H. Batchelder who has had dealings in bicycles for some time back, established the above concern January 1, 1895, and is doing a successful business. Mr. Batchelder is about 36 years of age. His partner is Mr. Frank E. Lewis. They handle the Fowler, Fenton, Warwick, Puritan and Ben Hurr bicycles, both ladies' and gentlemen's. All of the above machines are gaining a world wide reputation daily. The above concern continues to build up their reputation in and about the city of Lowell. This concern also makes a specialty of handling different parts and connections for bicycles and they have the best facilities for repairing, which is fast gaining the esteem and honor of Lowell's bicyclists, with its honorable record of the past 10 years. It still maintains a leading proportion in its line of trade.

MOXIE NERVE FOOD CO.,

21 Branch St.

It is safe to say that no article or compound, whether known as medicine food, or by any other name, has made such gigantic strides into popularity as has Moxie Nerve Food. The receipt for this compound has been in the possession of Dr. Augustine Thompson, of this city for several years, and it has been carefully tested by him in his private practice. It is safe to say that it is efficient for the cure or perversion of certain diseases, and it being thoroughly proven to him, he secured his present accommodations for the manufacture of the same. Time has proven the test and the doctor scarcely saw the phenomenal success so soon to be achieveu by it. A company was formed with the doctor at its head. A laboratory was established on Market street, near Worthen, and the manufacture was commenced, at what at that time was deemed a large scale. Soon, however, as its use became more and more known, the Market street quarters were found to be entirely too small and the vast building on Branch street, formerly used as a skating rink, was secured and all its extensive floor space and facilities, generally are devoted to the company's use. A number of branch factories have been established in different parts of the country, until there now exists scarce a city from Halifax to San Francisco where the medicine is unknown, or has not been used.

Twenty-four men and women and seven horses are kept busily employed by the Branch street factory, and the sales from this factory alone outnumbered the spring months of 1891, which amounted to nearly one hundred and seventy-eight thousand, eight hundred cases of medicine, and they have speedily increased ever since. All this great business is now handled by the doctor alone, and that all his energy might be devoted to it he gave up the entire local practice enjoyed by him in this city. Moxie is claimed not to be a stimulant but a nerve food, artificially digested and made ready for absorption before being taken into the system. This method of artificial absorption is a secret known only to the doctor, and one which skilled lawyers in court have been unable to make him divulge.

The doctor embodies two things necessary for success in all lines of business, a sound mind and a whole body. He was born in Union, Maine. At an early age he moved to Rockland in that state, and lived there until the breaking out of the war. He is as strong and sturdy as the pine tree of his native state. He enlisted in the army as a private. The same push and courage distinguished him that marked his subsequent career. Promotion came rapidly to him. Twice on the field being recommended by General Banks, and after being in 71 engagements, among them the assault on Port Hudson, he was mustered into the service with the rank of Lieutenant Colonel. After the war he practiced medicine in this city about 20 years. He is well informed, having traveled extensively. He is a man with ideas and has the courage to put them into practice.

The Moxie Company have recently put upon the market two more of Dr. Thompson's preparations, Moxie Catarrh Cure and Safe Guard, both in one package. The Catarrh Cure is used as a lady uses her smelling bottle; it is also a harmless and rich cologne. The Safe Guard, you take five of its tiny pellets on the tongue before retiring and it does away with the effects from exposure to colds and epidemic diseases. It is safe to use. The sales of these remedies for the short time they have been upon the market, have never been equaled in the history of the trade.

H. R. BARKER MANUFACTURING CO.

This firm was originally established 40 years ago by Mr. Barker. In the year 1887 it obtained the name of H. R. Barker Manufacturing Company, and was incorporated with the purpose in view of manufacturing steam heating apparatus and doing general machine work, a specialty in their work being gas fixtures and brass castings. Finding that this branch was increasing to such an extent as to require a great portion of their time they obtained the rest of the building which is situated on Middle street. This building is a four story structure of brick, where everything is compact and every inch of space of the room is utilized. The firm in the busy season employs a number of hands and personally, as far as possible, looks after the construction. They have also to their credit many examples of the economy of the proper use of steam heating devices. This establishment has been a very successful one since it was incorporated in 1887, in the line of water heating, steam heating, etc. The company has made a special study under the direction of Mr. Barker, and its new members have made successful examples of many public and private buildings under their direction of heating appliances. This firm is one of the prides of Lowell in being a successful plant operated in the above line of heating and ventilation.

L. C. HALL,

Storage, Hay and Straw, 631 Dutton St.

The leading and oldest established house for the purpose of storage is Mr. L. C. Hall's, whose place was established in 1870. He started business in a small but sure way, and is doing business to-day within 20 feet of the spot of his first location, which is directly across the street from No. 631 Dutton street. Since 1870 Mr. Hall has added to his already large storage rooms three massive buildings, where merchandise, furniture and storage of any and of all descriptions are placed with security, in fact it is well worthy of the name of "Security Storage." Mr. Hall owns it and gives ample security for all goods stored at his place.

Mr. Hall is 60 years of age, and it is well to say that he is the leading merchant in the storage line of business in this city. He has also in connection with the storage business, hay and straw, which he deals out in large bulk quantities. His business has annually increased since his beginning to a vast extent, and he is considered an energetic, wide awake, honorable business man, and anyone having relations with him will find him of the most attractive character. The enterprise is the leading factor in the economy of storage, and as it is operated adds greatly to the advantages of the city as a manufacturing center.

PARKER & HALL,

Wholesale Dealers in Cheese, Butter, Eggs and General Products.

This important and respected house is but three years old by the present owners. The house is at present conducted under the name of Parker & Hall at No. 598 Dutton street. It was founded about ten year's ago by Denning & Parker. Three years ago the present owners took possession and have since conducted the business in an energetic, practical business manner. The trade of the house extends throughout many of the counties surrounding the city of Lowell.

All stock is procured direct from the original sources of supply in large quantities, and is furnished to the trade at lowest market prices, shipments being also made to destination in large lots. The firm handle only reliable and well known brands of flour, and are agents only for the high brands which are manufactured from the choicest wheat. They handle cheese, butter and eggs, and the relations of the firm are such that choice consignments are received daily, and orders are filled with fresh superior goods.

JOHN TRIPP & CO.,

Manufacturer of all Kinds of Cotts, Rolls; Mills Dutton St.

It hardly requires us to describe the process of Roll Covering for the general reader would take in fact but little interest in it, or care to familiarize himself with the manner with which the process is obtained. The oldest Roll Covering establishment in Lowell is that of John Tripp & Company, founded by John Tripp in 1852. He began operations on a very small scale in the yard of the Massachusetts corporation. Mr. Tripp's death occurred in 1888, the business being continued under the name of J. Tripp & Company, conducted by Messrs. A. C. Pearsons and S. C. Wood, both being connected with the concern before Mr. Tripp's death. The interested parties in the company are A. C. Pearsons and Mrs. E. A. Mansur, who is a daughter of Mr. Tripp.

The works are now situated on the ground floor of the Mechanics Mills, Dutton street, occupying a floor space of about 40 by 80 feet which is completely occupied with Uewell Wyllys Machines and other modern appliances. They employ from 20 to 25 experts in their line of work. Their trade is not confined to the New England States, as deliveries are made to India and South Carolina. Those who are dissatisfied with the rolls which they are now using, are invited to send this company a sample order, which will receive immediate and careful attention. Where it is inconvenient to send rolls, the firm manufactures cuts of selected sheep and calf skins which can be had upon application at the mills. All work is guaranteed. For references we submit the following corporations who will vouch for their responsibility: Boott Cotton Mills, Massachusetts and Prescott Cotton Mills; Tremont and Suffolk Mills, the Lawrence Manufacturing Company, Appleton Company and Lowell Machine Shop, also Naumkeag Steam Engine Company, of Salem, Mass., and many others.

E. F. FERRIN,

Retail Highland Shoe Dealer.

The enterprise of Mr. Ferrin as a shoe merchant was established 15 years ago. He was then located in what is at present occupied by Talbot's Clothing Company. He conducted business there for about 10 years, at the expiration of which time he moved to the Highlands on Branch street, three doors from the corner of School street. He conducted business at that place for about four years, when he moved diagonally across the street to a corner location. At this place he conducts the same line of business with the addition of a bicycle department as a specialty.

Mr. Ferrin is about 39 years of age and has a wide experience in the shoe business in the city of Lowell. He is well known for his practical business experience and long standing as a merchant in the city of Lowell. He handles the Eclipse Bicycle as a side line, both ladies'and gentlemen's wheels. This department has been a thorough success. Too much cannot be said of Mr. Ferrin's character, both in social and in a business way. He is a progressive business man and his operation is based upon fair and reliable dealing. He is a great credit to the community established in the district of the Highlands.

N. J. WEIR & C.

The important enterprise of N. J. Weir & Company was originally established in the year of 1857, and it has since been managed by Mr. Weir himself. They have a substantial building situated on Market street, where they conduct their business. The line of goods consists of cooking stoves and ranges, light and heavy stove castings, grates and fire brick, tin ware and copper ware. This company enjoys a large patronage among the local residents of the city. They make delivery estimates upon all kinds of repairing, such as stove linings, legs, hearths, dampers, pipes, reservoirs, standards, kettles, boilers, etc. The company is one of the oldest of its kind in the city of Lowell. They can be depended upon as a most reliable and practical business concern.

P. J. BOLAND,

Expert Horse Shoer, No. 978 Middlesex St.

Mr. Boland has been in the blacksmith business but four years, and he is considered by horse owners as an expert horse shoer for trotting, interfering and over-reaching horses. He is 27 years of age. He has been located at No. 978 Middlesex street for the past four years. He occupies a wooden structure having a floor space of about 30 or 40 feet, with large double doors, with two entrances, making a cool spot for the skilful operation of shoeing valuable horses. Mr. Boland is not only skilful himself but employs only skilled workmen. He is said to be perfect in the execution of his work. He makes a specialty of shoeing fast horses at reasonable prices.

WOOD'S,

Jewelry, Watches, Silver Ware and Optics of all Kinds.

This widely known establishment is now about to complete a half-century's existence. It was founded over 25 years ago in a small store on Central street, by Geo. Wood. This well known house is located at No. 143 to 151 Central street, and has a 50 foot plate glass front. When Mr. Wood began business he had but two narrow plate windows, with but one show case. Today he has 11 show cases. His usual number of clerks is 12, but in the busy season he employs many more. This concern has

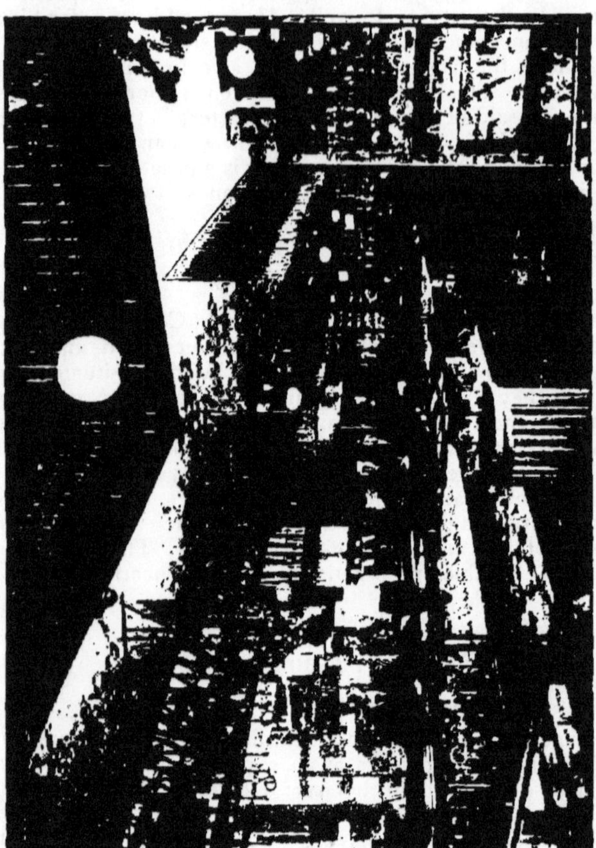
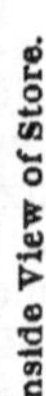

Inside View of Store.

attained popularity and has become widely known as one of the most reliable houses in Lowell. An optical department in this establishment embraces the most improved and modern character of tasteful appliances, which is in charge of a thoroughly competent optician. The firm not only handles jewelry, but imported clocks, lamps, silver ware, lodge and organization pins and emblems, and also makes jewelry to order. The store is richly made up in the interior, and the elegant show cases display their contents of the vast variety of specialties. The establishment comprises one of the notable and important factors of the industrial supremacy of this thriving city.

J. BAKER,

Fancy Goods, Worsteds, Yarns, etc.

Successor to Alice Brown. The enterprise of J. Baker, situated in the Fiske building of this city, ranks second to none of its kind in America, for they have a history which dates back half a century, it having changed hands but three times in the elapse of 50 years. There has been a constant demand for the superior products which they handle, in the ciiy of Lowell, and it is increasing in volume continually. The line embraces worsteds, yarns, cottons, silks and every imaginary fancy working material. The present large stock is handled by Mr. Baker and two competent ladies, who understand their line of work thoroughly. Mr. Baker still maintains his prominent position in this useful and valuable industry, and its marked growth and success is alike creditable to its management. The doors have never been closed on any account or reason within the past above history, excepting on legal holidays, Sundays and on one other occasion. It is the only line of business of its kind in the city of Lowell, where they give their whole attention to the sale of worsteds, yarns, silks and fancy articles of every description. Mr. Baker is known to the trade as a broad guage and progressive business man, anxious to provide the public of Lowell with the most advanced accommodations in his line of business.

GEORGE FAIRBURN,

Merrimack Market.

There is no establishment in Lowell that shows more conclusively the rapid advancement and improvements made in the line of meats, vegetables, cheese, eggs, fruit, canned goods, and a variety of delicacies. The elegant and luxurious inside fixtures located in the center isle give great facilities for the display of the different styles of goods and meats, in an immense long glass refrigerator. Mr. Fairburn began business when he was but 14 years of age in Lancashire, England. He came to Lowell in 1880 and has since owned and managed the Quincy Market in Centralville. He was located there four years, but is now located at 20 Merrimack street, and conducts the business there under the name of Merrimack Square Market. It is impossible to find a more finely furnished or better equipped interior outside of the metropolis. All its departments are of the most perfect type of modern art. Mr. Fairburn is 31 years of age, has an excellent business experience, and understands his line from beginning to end. He requires the services of seven clerks and four delivery teams. He is in quick touch with the cheese and market centers, and displays fine specimens of all niceties in his line, in the latest and most novel way. The public of Lowell will find both Mr. Fairburn and his numerous clerks the most congenial and courteous people to deal with.

S. C. PATRICK,

Wholesale and Retail Cigar Dealer and Manufacturer.

The enterprise of S. C. Patrick was established in the year of 1853, and he has since built up a trade that places him in the front rank of tobac-

J.C.AYER CO

conists in Lowell. It is the only strictly wholesale and retail house, of the age and history of over half a century, existing, and its trade extends throughout a half dozen surrounding counties. The premises occupied for the business are large and commodious, the floor comprising a space about 40 feet square, which is used for small storage and salesroom and for storing finished stock. Mr. Patrick is now over 70 years of age, his hair being quite white. He is somewhat bent with the many years of toil and labor by which he has attained the extensive business now located on Prescott street. Of late years he has not employed many cigar makers and assistants on account of his age which caused him to pay more attention to his health. Today he is ranked among the leading and respected firms of the city of Lowell. The firm also carries a complete stock of manufactured cigarettes and smokers' articles for the trade which are offered at manufacturers' prices. He makes a specialty of repairing fine pipes, and he is a man who is practically acquainted with every detail in his line of business, giving it his personal supervision.

J. C. AYER CO.

Jacob Rogers, President; Frederick Ayer, Treasurer—Proprietors and Manufacturers of Ayer's Sarsaparilla, Ayer's Cherry Pectoral, Ayer's Hair Vigor, Ayer's Ague Cure, and Ayer's Cathartic Pills—Laboratory, Market Street. Office and Warehouse, No. 98 Middle Street—See Illustration on Opposite Page.

The aspiration to relieve and remedy human suffering is a noble one, and when that aspiration is seconded by intelligent, well-directed effort, the results attained entitle the laborer to the appellation of philanthropist. This is especially true in the field of medicine—a profession which has contributed to the annals of the race such deathless names as Jenner, Pasteur, Koch and MacKenzie. Equally with these—perhaps in an even greater degree—the name of Ayer is worthy of honor, while there is no question that among the masses of mankind it is far better known and more affectionately regarded than that of either of the illustrious investigators and discoverers first referred to. James Cook Ayer was born at Groton, Conn., May 5, 1818, attended the common school there, and afterward took a course at the Westford (Mass.) academy. From 1838 to 1842 he was clerk and student of pharmacy in the drugstore of Jacob Robbins of Lowell, studied medicine at a later period with Dr. Samuel L. Dana, and was eventually graduated with the degree of M. D. by the University of Pennsylvania. Meanwhile, in April, 1841, he purchased the Robbins drugstore, and developed by investigation and experiment the now world-famous Cherry Pectoral, the success of which as a specific for coughs, colds, lung and throat troubles rendered the subsequent introduction of his later preparations a comparatively easy matter, such is the prestige of an initial triumph fairly won. Dr. Ayer's first removal was from Central street to the present *Mail* building, and in June, 1855, his brother Frederick became associated with him and the style Dr. Ayer & Co. was adopted by the new firm. In 1872 Dr. J. C. Ayer & Co. bought a plot of land in the rear of the laboratory and fronting on Middle street—the site of the old Green schoolhouse—and erected thereon a large office and warehouse structure, bridges spanning the railroad track and connecting the two buildings. The new premises served their purpose very well

VIEW IN MAIN OFFICE.

until a year or two ago, when the J. C. Ayer Company (organized and incorporated Oct. 24, 1877, capital $300,000) added one story and a modern business front to this edifice, making it five stories in height, with a total of over 44,000 square feet in area, and one of the most attractive and commodious, as well as most elegantly fitted and convenient commercial blocks in New England. The office alone affords 7360 square feet of floorage, and is a vast hive of business, no less than sixty male and female clerks, stenographers, type-writers, book-keepers and managers of departments being employed there, under the experienced and watchful eye of Mr. Frederick Ayer, the treasurer, who, though advanced in years, is fully capable of performing the labors and carrying the responsibilities that devolve upon him. We feel that our description of this mammoth concern is inadequate in the matter of details, but plead lack of space as our excuse, for nothing would please us better than to delineate *in extenso* each department and the operations carried on therein. We may add, however, that the J. C. Ayer Company leases the big brick block adjoining the laboratory on Market street, where are stored vast quantities of raw materials, paper, bottles, etc.; that they employ in all over 250 people, and that they are the leading manufacturers of proprietary medicines in the world, their unrivaled Sarsaparilla, Cherry Pectoral, Hair Vigor, Ague Cure and Cathartic Pills being as well known and as popular in the remotest quarters of the globe as in the most enlightened portions of Europe and America.

LOWELL & SUBURBAN RAILROAD CO.,

General Offices Corner of Merrimack and Prescott Sts.

One of the first pleasant impressions made upon the mind of a stranger upon alighting from the cars is the extensive and convenient street railway system, furnishing rapid transit and close connection which are fully equal with those of the most advanced metropolitan centers, and far ahead of the majority in many respects. Not the least noticeable is the cleanness of the cars, the courtesy of the employes in charge, and the long distance to which passengers are conveyed.

The line reaches from the business center of the city in all available directions and extends to the most distant manufacturing districts, as well as to the suburban cities and towns of Billerica, North Chelmsford, Chelmsford Centre, Pawtucketville, Dracut, Collinsville and the summer resorts of Lakeview, Willow Dale and Mountain Rock. There is under construction now a plant to be operated between Nashua, New Hampshire, and Lowell, connections being made at Lakeview. The entire railroad is operated by electric power. The Lowell, Lawrence & Haverhill road also operates a road between those cities, making trips in both directions about every half hour.

The Lowell & Suburban Company are extending their lines every season in all directions to the environs. Having anticipated the needs of the public, in whatever direction a citizen may live he will find close car connections in most any district of the city. The fare to the summer resorts is but five cents; in the city limits five cents with transfers.

W. A. INGHAM,

Wholesale Produce Grocer and Merchant, No. 44 Church Street.

This important and representative house, if not the oldest of its kind, the leading one of today, and one which still remains at the head of its affairs, is that of W. A. Ingham & Company.

Mr. Ingham first established the grocery business in 1865 in the Wamesit Bank building on Middlesex street; conducted business in that place until 1879, at which time he entered the telephone business in this city as a successful speculator, promoter and stock financier, in which he became a very prominent figure throughout the United States. In 1885 he engaged in his first business in partnership with Ralph Bradbury, at which time the well-known Ingham block was built in 1890. This building has many fine features, being a five story brick structure embracing about three quarters of an acre floor space, having an elevator run by electric power the size of which is about nine by fifteen (9 by 15) feet and is of the latest design, carrying a capacity of great weight and being run by a fifteen-horse power motor. The building has no less than one hundred and seventy-five windows and it can be said that it is one of the lightest buildings in the city of Lowell. It is especially adapted to the five particular lines to which it is devoted, namely: Wholesale, Liquor, Bookbinding, Wall Paper, Wholesale Groceries and Lowell Electric Light Company's office. It also has large access at both front and rear to the freight house of the B. & M. R. R., being directly opposite, which makes the receiving and shipping of merchandise very handy.

W. A. Ingham is 53 years of age, born in the state of Maine and served two years and a half in the service. All the stock is procured direct from the ordinary sources of supply in large quantities, which enables him to furnish to the trade all goods at the lowest market rates. Shipments are also made to destination without re-handling. The firm handles only reliable and well recognized brands of every article which the retail trade have demand for. Mr. Ingham came to Lowell in 1860, penniless, with a small box containing all his belongings, which he has decorated at present, with the word upon it "Success."

JOHN BOWERS & SONS

Is the name under which the proprietorship of the famous summer resort, "Willow Dale," located about six miles out of Lowell, is known; it is connected by a system of electric cars operated from both Lowell and Nashua, New Hampshire.

This romantic and historic place is situated on the east side of a handsome lake the width of which is about one mile, directly opposite of Mountain Rock and northeast of Lakeview. The attention of the public is called to the numerous relics which adorn the verandas, piazza, dining room, dance hall, grove and grounds in general of fine sculpture work of many famous artists, among which is a statue of General Jackson standing over twelve feet high from the base.

Mr. John Bowers who died recently left many small relics of his collection which are on exhibition at Willow Dale. The business is now conducted by John and George Bowers, sons of the above named, who are also manufacturers of the widely known "Willow Dale chips," and conduct a wholesale and retail business at 218 Merrimack street, Lowell, Mass. The manner in which Willow Dale is conducted makes it a more desirable resort than many of the better known places, commanding only the better class of trade for their summer cottages and daily patrons, and it is safe to say that the coming career of Willow Da'e will surpass any in the vicinity in the near future. The entrance to Willow Dale is handsomely arched with stone. At this entrance a steamboat can be boarded which carries all passengers to Willow Dale centre, where everything of an enjoyable nature can be found; handsome drives, bathing, boating, fishing, sailing, dancing, singing, swinging, bowling, merry-go-rounds and band concerts. The dining hall is furnished with all the delicacies of the season.

THE MORRILL—WESCOTT STUDIO,

Central Block.

The studio of Robert E. Wescott was built for and established by F. F. Morrill in 1881, whose fame as an expert in his line and especially as an artist became very widespread. He studied under Vickery of Haverhill and others. He is perhaps better known for his exquisite effects in the then new Carbon process than in any other line.

In 1891 the business was taken by Mr. Wescott, who had studied under Mr. Morrill and elsewhere in New England, as well as under Hill, the renowned Asbury Park, N. J., photographer. Mr. Morrill left some 20-000 negotiations which are carefully stored and registered at the studio in remarkably complete alphabetical order. This collection (including many of the representative people of Lowell and its environs) has been largely increased during the four years in which Mr. Wescott has had charge of it, and forms a very valuable and interesting feature of the studio. All the effects of lighting, etc., have been recently renovated in conformity with the very sensitive weather which forms one of the essentials of modern science in both chemical and optical lines.

Mr. Wescott's success with children is perhaps a point that may be mentioned in connection with the place and several entirely new styles of pictures have recently been introduced by him, including the "Princess," the success of which has been quite remarkable.

The free art gallery connected with the studio has held practically all the large collections of high class paintings in Lowell, in recent years. Among the exhibitions may be mentioned W. P. Phelps, whose Munich pictures created such a furore when he returned from that art center, and whose more recent works near his favorite Mt. Monadnock have become such a feature of the American art world.

Sears Gallaghar, the noted illustrator of Boston, Alfred Ordaw, the ex-curator of the Boston Art Club, H. P. Greaves, the special artist of the B. & M. R. R., and among the many local artists, P. I. Coggeshall, whose marines attract praise and attention wherever exhibited, and J. A. Nesmith, whose charming water colors are rapidly becoming known to our art lovers.

This feature of the studio provides a long felt want in the city. During the winter months a "life class" containing several of the above gentlemen and many others who will be heard from later, hold weekly talks in the studio and by mutual criticism assist each other and gain much benefit.

To return to photography, Mr. Wescott strives rather for the artistic than the new and momentarily pleasing results, believing that a reputation founded upon artistic merit is more desirable than temporary fame. The studio is easy of access, being supplied with excellent elevator services; is commodious and centrally located, and has for many years held an enviable reputation for its superior class of patronage.

A. O. AUSTIN,

Bicycles, Bicycle Attachments and Repair Shop, 115 Paige St.

Among the most reliable houses of the city of Lowell is the establishment of A. O. Austin who is agent for the Phœnix bicycle and located at No. 115 Paige street. Mr. Austin established his place in 1892 and evidently it has grown to be a very successful business. The premises occupied for the business are fitted up with the most modern style of machinery for rapid repairs, etc.

Mr. Austin makes a specialty of building bicycles to order. He has a very central location and employs a number ot skilled hands in his repair and supply department; altogether the resources and facilities of the house are thoroughly equal in every respect to those of dealers in the metropolis, and the most advanced methods are in force, which gives the greatest inducements to the trade. His enterprise has done its full share toward attracting to Lowell that trade which owing to its central position is unsurpassed.

POSTAL TELEGRAPH-CABEL CO.

In 1887 the Commercial Union Telegraph Co. extended its system to Lowell, its first office being equipped with four wires to Boston. The amount of business done was small, but gradually increased until Jan. 1, 1893, when the Postal Telegraph-Cable Co. leased the property and rebuilt and enlarged all the lines. Lowell was made a junction point, with 12 wires to Boston, 4 to Albany, 4 to Concord and 8 to Portland. The service is now first-class in every respect, and its reliability and celerity has earned for it the confidence of the public.

The Postal Co. is the largest and only successful competitive system ever maintained. The management has from the first determined to establish a permanent business, based on sound principles and business-like methods, and has steadfastly adhered to that policy. Its employees are intelligent, diligent, energetic and enthusiastic. They are in sympathy with their employers, and aim to give the best telegraph service. The Postal building in New York, which is shown in the above cut, is the most perfectly arranged telegraph office in the world, and cost over $1,000,000.

The Postal Co., was the first to use typewriters in connection with the telegraph, and was the first company to adopt the dynamo current for telegraphic purposes in place of the old style batteries.

The system embraces 5,000 offices, with two distinct routes from the

Atlantic to the Pacific; and is operated in connection with the Commercial Cable Co., having three cables to Europe. This is the Cable Co through whose instrumentality the cable-rates were cut down, and kept down, from 40 cents to 25 cents per word.

The Lowell office is now conveniently located at 15 Central street.

PETER FINNEGAN,

Merrimack House Barber Shop.

This enterprise was surely a common factor of the city of Lowell, it having a record of over 23 years existence. Mr. Finnegan was born in Lowell in 1878. In 1890 he established a barber shop in the old Post Office Block. In 1873 he moved to his present quarters in the American House Block, where he has since been located. Without a doubt this is the finest barber shop in the New England states, the proprietor being most courteous toward patrons; his assistants are extremely polite and on that account he is rapidly increasing the number of his patrons daily.

MOWER & SPARKS.

This concern has been established but a very short time, but having two active industrial business men conducting it, it is speedily increasing in prominence daily.

It can be said of both members of the firm that they are practical jewelers and engravers who understand their business. They have a central location at 185 Central St., where they make a specialty of the following goods; Watches, jewelry, diamonds, silverware of all description, clocks, pins, emblems and repairing of every description in their line. It is safe to say that this concern with their practical personal management and ability to push, will be a leading house in the future.

JAMES McCARRON,

Tea, Coffee, Etc.

The establishment of James McCarron was established Febuary, 1895, in the most prominent spot in the city, opposite the new postoffice, number 44 Gorham street. Mr. McCarron is one of the fast growing wholesale and retail tea and coffee merchants of Lowell, and he extends a call to the public in giving his teas and coffees a trial. He claims he can suit where others fail. His line embraces Rio, Mocha and Java Coffees, Japan, Oolong, English Breakfast, Black Tea, and Young Hesin. Every pound of tea delivered by the above house is entitled to a ticket. When a certain number is reached the ticket entitles the purchaser to a present in some line of crockery, which is on exhibition there daily.

Mr. McCarron gives the business his personal management and he is sure of success in the manner in which the business is conducted. He has first-class delivering facilities and a prompt service attending to customers. His prices are right and in harmony with quality. A trial of his goods will result in ample satisfaction. This young enterprising house has many advantageous relations, and is in a position to furnish the public with teas, coffees, spices, etc., at the most remarkable prices available.

BUTTRICK & CO.

Market St.

An account of the business of Lowell will be hardly complete had it not a mention of this concern, which was established in 1820 under the present name. It has continued from one generation to another and is now as then placed among the accepted leaders in the grocery trade in Lowell.

The names of John A. Buttrick, Abner Buttrick, Alden Buttrick, Benjamin N. Webber, Charles T. Goddard, all retired members of the firm, are well known and remembered by the oldest and most conservative business men with a degree of respect, which could only be attained by strict adherence to these principles of fair dealings and good goods which have always been maintained in this establishment.

In March, 1892, owing to death the business came into the possession of the present owners, H. P. Goodell and W. N. Goodell, who decided that the store must be put into more modern shape to fully accord with the demands of its patrons, and accordingly a complete renovation was undertaken and carried through, resulting in a store second to none in New England. And the renovation affected not only the store but the stock as well, for when reopened there was added an assortment of imported and domestic delicacies which recorded with the "up-to-date" appearance of the place of business, and today there are few stores, outside of Boston, so completed and well assorted.

A special feature is the "Golden Sheaf" flour of which many barrels are distributed monthly, and it ranks superior to any other brand. The tea and coffee trade is one which needs most careful attention and it is a large and important branch of the business and one which, judging from the steady increase, has catered satisfactorily to the wants of the discriminating public.

One little item in many groceries is almost lost sight of; it is cheese, which with this firm assumes an importance second to none. At almost any private house, club, hotel or restaurant you will find served some of "Buttrick & Co.'s" cheese.

Butter is also a line of importance, especially the product of the Whiting Creamery which is received fresh every day, in addition to which are many brands of both creamery and dairy, in all shapes and sizes. There is no other line that stands forth with more prominence than butter or cheese. It would make a bulky folio if we started to tell of the many delicacies which can be found at this store, but it is sufficient to say, "You can depend on it if it came from Buttrick's."

WILLARD H. GOODFELLOW, SR.,

Inventor and Publisher.

A short and interesting history is that of W. H. Goodfellow, Sr., possibly the youngest man in Lowell who has the honor of having senior attached to his name, for he is scarcely 24 years of age, and we give a little of his business career.

He was born in the city of New Haven, state of Connecticut, and when a young boy of about 7 years of age his folks moved to the city of Troy, N. Y.; he received a public school education, and while at school one afternoon in July in the year of 1881, there was being auctioned off a span of goats with a miniature turnout. Having just been released from school he wandered down town, bid upon the goats, and the auctioneer having reached his third bid, the boy received the goats for $9.75. But before paying for the same he ordered the span driven to the leading hat and gent's furnishing house, applied for a position in connection with the goats, that he might advertise their business nights after school. At first the proprietor could see no use in the boy's suggestion, and declined to give him any attention. When the boy was about to leave the store he called him back and made arrangement with him, after considering the subject, for $4.00 per week and support of the goats. He immediately took the boy by the hand, led him to the nearest tailor shop, ordered a complete livery outfit and silk hat for the boy. He worked for about six months for a remuneration of $4.00 a week, when he thought his income was not quite large enough. The boy then solicited customers for 60 quarts of milk to be delivered in the city, which he conducted between the hours of 3 and 7 o'clock in the morning. He carried on the milk business in connection with his advertising enterprise for about six months longer. He then contrived and managed someway to utilize the hours between 7 and school hours, which was 9 o'clock, to solicit customers by which he could use his goats in delivering nine baskets of collars for the collar factories and return them to the parties for whom he worked. He then went to school and utilized his regular time constantly for three years, working after school for the firm of Stamper & Strait of the above city. When he reached the age of 13 he thought himself too large to ride in a miniature turnout, and he sold the same to parties in Williamstown, Mass., for about five times the amount paid for them at the auction.

Mr. Strait, a partner of the above concern, became attached to the boy and while in New York buying goods in the year of 1884, bought a handsome black pony and miniature cab, and Mr. Goodfellow conducted his regular business of advertising, milk and collar routes the same as usual for another year, when one day while coming down a steep hill, the horse being one of the fiery species, became frightened and dashed down the hill with the boy, who came out of the catastrophe with nothing broken but his hat. The horse and cab were damaged considerably. The boy then went to work in the store as clerk in the straw hat department, working day times and attending night school, still conducting his other lines. The following year he became promoted and took charge of the stiff hat department, and in his 19th year he had an idea of going West, and wrote a letter to one of the largest concerns in the city of Detroit, the firm of Mabley & Co , and on the following Friday left Troy, N. Y., for that city, where the concern gave him a week's trial in their hat department. The following week resulted in a promotion to assistant manager, which position he held for one year. Shortly after the general manager died, and he was placed in his position. His department had no less than 27 clerks and a large number of check boys. He was married at the age of 20 and today has two sons.

Mr. Goodfellow is now 24 years of age and is a partner in the firm of Goodfellow-Bowers Co., Electric Car Improvement Manufacturers, is interested in a local manufacturing company, and is the inventor of a number of car improvements. Mr. Goodfellow is a well known, active citizen and is progressive and extremely eager to attain a high standard in a business career.

The offices of the company of Goodfellow-Bowers are located at 6 and 7 O'Donnell & Gilbride building, where a number of electrical car improvements are on exhibition.

J. W. BROOKS,

Undertaker, Embalmer and Funeral Director.

This prominent and popular undertaking establishment was established in 1862 by J. W. Brooks on Gorham street, and it is probably one of the oldest houses of the kind in the city of Lowell. Mr. Brooks was born in Lynn, Mass., in 1836. He has been a constant business man in the city of Lowell for 39 years past, at his first location on Prescott street, he was but a few years when he moved to number 16 Market street, where he has conducted the undertaking business ever since. This house finds it essential to use three horses and wagons in their business.

No house in the city has a finer reputation in character, honorable, straight, upright dealings, than that of J. W. Brooks. Mr. Brooks has great executive faculties in directing funerals; he is also a very conservative and effective business manager, and has become a leading factor in the general business prosperity of this section of the country.

J. M. SPURR,

Shirt Manufacturing Co.

This company is an old, representative house in their line of business, having been established since 1869, their first location being number 65 Market street. In 1877 they moved to No. 35 Shattuck street, where they have since conducted the manufacture of Custom Shirts, Collars and Cuffs. They are the most reliable custom shirt makers in the city of Lowell.

Mr. Spurr is 54 years of age and his long experience in the business gives him a wide reputation as a thorough, practical shirt maker and designer. His line embraces custom made, white negligees, and every description of wearing apparel used for the above purposes.

This house has a general advantage in buying goods direct from the manufacturer of the materials. They are in close touch with the manufacturers which enables them to take advantage of new patterns, designs, qualities, etc. As to the reliability and honorable dealings of this firm comment would be pertinent, as its high standing and magnitude of operation is ample evidence of the character of its business policy.

DAVIS & SARGENT.

This is an old-established and reliable concern, founded by Otis Allen in 1848. Stephen C. Davis succeeded Mr. Allen in 1869, and the present firm was organized upon the admission of Mr. B. F. Sargent in 1872. The plant comprises a one-story and basement saw-mill, 50 x 100 feet, on the Pawtucket Canal, and a fine two and three story brick planing-mill and factory. The Davis & Sargent block fronting on Middlesex street, connected with which is a three story warehouse and office building, a number of sheds, etc., the yards lying between the saw and planing mill and adjacent to both. The equipment of both mills is first class and the productive capacity is very large, sixty hands finding steady employment on the premises, while two steam engines of 100 horse power each drive the machinery. The firm carries large stocks of choice white and yellow pine, spruce, hemlock, white wood and hardwood lumber, which will be delivered in the rough or dressed to order for the trade. Dimension timbers also are prepared as required, and builders and others supplied with every description of flooring, clapboards, shingles, etc. A specialty is made of packing boxes for corporations and medicines, water closets, tanks, etc., and manufacturers can have their orders filled here to any extent, at short notice and on reasonable terms. The saw-mill on the canal is the only one in Lowell making direct from the log, and turns out over 3,000 000 feet per annum, about 2,500,000 feet of which is worked up in the adjoining shops. The logs come from New Hampshire via the Merrimack River and the canal.

Messrs. Davis & Sargent are both natives of New Hampshire, and Mr. Davis was with Mr. Allen from 1852 until he became sole owner in 1866. They own the four story brick block, which is 45 x 180 feet, on Middlesex street, which they rent to small industrial concerns, furnishing steam when needed.

W. P. & R. F. BRAZER,

Hats, Gent's Furnishings, Bicycle Goods, Etc.

Nothing shows better the steady prominent advance which Lowell is making as a business center and the character of the blocks and stores built for business purposes than the Mansur Block. During the past few years the progress toward a fine class of structures has been constant, and the result is that our three principal streets are lined with structures that would not be out of place in a metropolis. The oldest house receiving this attention is the Mansur building at the corner of Central and Market streets. It has no doubt been described before, but we take pleasure to dwell upon the description a moment, and simply desire to call attention to a single feature of the block, which is the very successful firm of W. P. & R. F. Brazer.

Messrs. Brazer first moved into it in 1842. Their predecessor was Amos Rugg, who was preceded by E. D. Leavitt; the block itself was built by Aaron Mansur, father of Mrs. J. Nesmith, in 1834. He was very prominent in the work of building the town and far-seeing in his real estate investments. Mr. Mansur also built up a good name for integrity and uprightness more lasting than business structures, and his death in 1859 was a source of regret to the community.

The offices over the store have been the business habitation of many eminent lawyers and well known citizens among whom were: Hon. Joel Adams, Clippan Duckworth, J. W. Mansur, Isaac S. Morse, J. W. Beard, Judge J. G. Abbott, George Stevens, Samuel T. Haven, R. G. Colby, Granville Parker, Sheriff Varnum and Deputy Butterfield, Pease and Bancroft. and many others of importance.

The quarters of W. P. & R. F. Brazer at present is one of the finest of its line in the city of Lowell, and it is superior in everything that goes to make it a pleasant store to trade in. Not one like it will be found in the country. It occupies the room of Brazer's old store and Hapgood & Wright's shoe store. It strikes one on entering as a bright and beautiful place and the tone of its finish impresses one favorably. The entire finish is in harmony with the effect of the great amount of glass work in the store, which is simply elegant. All the fittings are in keeping with the modern progress of its management, and since their first location they have taken in number 12 Market street which adds to their floor space about 60 x 15 feet of room in the rear to the already large floor room. At the right is the revolving arrangement for canes and umbrellas and on the north and west sides are the shelves and drawers devoted to hats with neat tables on which they are displayed for inspection. On the left again in rear of the front window is the collar and cuff department, further along the hosiery and shirt departments with the finest of display show cases in the center, and the fine office which was located in the center of the store is moved back to the left hand corner as you enter. The show case contents are displayed at night by large incandescent lights.

Down stairs, which has the same floor space as the main floor, is stored the heavy stock of reserved goods. In the rear is located their straw hat department and bicycle goods, of which they make a specialty, with robes, hammocks, underwear, etc.

CHADWICK & ARNOLD,

Cigar Manufacturers, Importers of Smokers' Articles.

One of the leading factors in the cigar line in Lowell is the firm of Chadwick & Arnold, successors to J. M. Joy & Co., whose history dates back many years. The above individuals took possession and established their personal character with the business Feb. 1, 1891.

Mr. Chadwick is a native of New York state, Mr. Arnold of Maine. They are both young, enterprising, "up-to-date" merchants in every particular, both being practical cigar makers, and their business is under their personal supervision constantly. The store, salesroom, factory and storage is located at No. 13 Central street, opposite the American House. This firm manufactures the cigar entitled "Old Comrade" which is no doubt the finest cigar outside of the metropolis; also the C. & A. ten cent cigar; a large distributing agency for Hurt & Co., Fifth Ave. ten cent cigar.

This firm have a very commodious factory and store on a prominent street directly opposite the American House, which is a three story building of brick structure. The business is systematically conducted by the two partners. A complete stock of cigars, jobbers' and smokers' articles are kept in goodly supply. In the factory ample accommodations are provided for storing the large stock of the different cigars which are constantly carried by the firm. All the cigars are manufactured and packed under special brands, the C. & A. sale being phenomenal.

Both Messrs. Chadwick and Arnold are experienced manufacturers and progressive business men, and they are actively identified with the industrial development of Lowell. They are expert selectors of leaf tobacco. Liberal and honest business methods is the motto under which their trade has been established, therefore, the reputation of this house is unsurpassed, and today it stands in the front rank of the important factors of Lowell's industries.

JAMES MURPHY & SON,

Insurance, Real Estate and Collectors.

One of the oldest commercial enterprises in the line of Real Estate, Insurance and Collecting Agencies is that of James Murphy, now James Murphy & Son, who are located at No. 15 Central street.

Mr. James Murphy has been in the Real Estate business for the past 15 years, having had his first location at the corner of Appleton and Gorham streets for eight years, after which time he moved to his present location on Central street. Eight years ago he added to the name of the concern Frank Brown Murphy, who is a son of Mr. Murphy. This change added to the firm's facilities for carrying on and conducting the business of Insurance, Underwriting, Real Estate and Collecting Agency. The members of the firm are experienced and enterprising business men who are closely identified with the development of the commercial supremacy of Lowell. The enterprise is an important one and fully deserves the highest esteem in which it is held by the public of Lowell.

They are both upright, fair, square, up to the point sort of men in all their business transactions. They enjoy unsurpassed facilities for handling all Real Estate and the collecting of bills.

NICHOLS & CO.,

Jobbers in Tea, Coffee, Spices, Etc.

A leading and prominent representative of the wholesale tea, coffee and spice jobbing house in Lowell is the firm of Nichols & Co., which was originally established in 1870 at the corner of Prescott and Merrimack

streets under the name of China Tea Co., being the first tea store in Lowell. Charles Nichols, the manager worked for the Oriental Tea Co., of Boston, before coming to Lowell, and had a wide experience in the tea and spice business, in fact has had a life long experience with the tea, coffee and spice business. Since their conducting a wholesale department the house has speedily advanced and a large and annually increasing trade has been developed that extends throughout surrounding communities, including New Hampshire. Vermont and Western Massachusetts, and entails the services of several traveling salesmen who visit Nashua, Concord, Laconia, Haverhill, Lawrence and other cities East. This is really the only wholesale tea and coffee house which strictly handles that line entirely in Lowell. They test each case of tea and coffee received before the goods are offered to the trade. In all departments of the business most advanced methods prevail, and the most complete facilities are placed at the disposal of customers. This firm has a direct connection with foreign markets; the advantages of a quick outlet for goods and the reliability of the house is such as to assure prompt returns for all consignments.

CLARENCE REYNOLDS,

Dye House, Prescott St.

Clarence A. Reynolds is the proprietor of the Bay State Dye House, having established his business here in 1886 and having obtained the name of the only responsible, practical, thorough dye house in the city of Lowell.

Mr. Reynolds came from the city of Worcester where he conducted the same business for years before. He is a practical dyer in every department of his line. His department requires the assistance of ten to twelve girls at present, but in the busy season it doubles that number usually. Mr. Reynolds was burnt out a short time ago, but like the progressive hustler that he is, is ready for business again at his old stand.

New machinery has been placed in the establishment which are labor saving articles of necessity to his line of business. Attention is also given to particular shades of dyeing and cleaning of every description of materials. Satisfaction is guaranteed by this responsible house to its patrons in every instance.

JOHN J. CLUIN,

Jeweler and Optician.

A successful business house is that of Hon. J. J. Cluin, which is located on Central street, near the junction of Prescott and at the head of Market street. Mr. Cluin is a successful business man, a prominent society man, and has long been known as a liberal, public spirited citizen of his adopted city, and most of his success has been won in Lowell. The Hub claims the honor of being his birthplace. Mr. Cluin was born in Boston, 36 years ago, on the 9th day of September, 1859. He learned his trade as a watchmaker and jeweler at the works of the Waltham Watch Co., under James N. Hammond, who was for 30 years with the American Waltham Co., and for 18 years foreman of the repair and adjusting department. To Mr. Hammond's training and experience Mr. Cluin owes his entire business success. He engaged in the jewelry business in Lowell in 1881, and from the start he made a splendid success. His finely appointed store is the center of attraction for a large and busy throng during business hours. He is a practical optician in connection with his jewelry business, and goods in that line can also be had and prices are guaranteed as cheap as in the metropolis.

This house is a live factor of the industries in Lowell and the pushing management of Mr. Cluin is sufficient to guarantee success to any business. His line embraces diamonds, watches, silverware, clocks and watch repairing and an optical department which is a special feature.

EMMA KITTREDGE,

Shorthand School, Central Block.

Miss Emma Kittredge, appreciating the value of a school in Lowell where stenography and typewriting could be thoroughly learned and students fitted for a business career, opened the Lowell Stenographic Institute in Central Block which she has successfully conducted for several years, and many of her graduates are now holding responsible positions as court stenographers and amanuenses.

After Miss Kittredge's marriage, she gave up her duties as a teacher and the school was closed for a short time, but in the fall of '94 Miss M. A. Goodale assumed the management and the school was reopened; but finding the duties too arduous for one, she has taken as her assistant Miss Julia Rafter, and by their painstaking attention and the superiority of the Allen System of shorthand (of which Miss Goodale is the only teacher in Lowell), the school has not only been brought to its former high standard but has reached a plane of efficiency second to none in the state.

Every attention is given to fitting pupils for a business life and a branch of the institute to which particular attention is given is the matter of special stenographic reporting at meetings, lectures, trials, etc.

GOODALE'S DRUG STORE,

217 Central St., Fiske Block.

The popularity of Goodale's drug store, which is situated at the corner of Central and Jackson streets, has been accomplished by strict attention to business and its well known policy of selling cheap. The fact that Goodale's drug store is the best place to trade is familiarly impressed on the minds of most people. Their popular low prices for different medicines are taken advantage of, as their sales will prove; not only on patent medicines do they make a saving, but on all articles found in a first-class drug store, especially so on prescriptions: they make a specialty of physicians' prescriptions and their facilities are unsurpassed by any other store in the city.

The rapid increase in their prescription trade compel them to have more help in order to accommodate their many patrons. Hereafter will be found four registered druggists in attendance and patrons can rely on prompt and courteous treatment.

CHARLES H. HANSON, JR.,

Manufacturer of Fine Harnesses and Saddlery, Corner of Fletcher and Dutton St.

This reputable house is a source of supply in this section of the country for horse owners. Charles H. Hanson began his business career at the age of 14 years, and discontinued it about 10 years later on account of ill health. At that time the firm name was C. H. Hanson & Co. Four years later he assumed the management of the harness and horse furnishing store which was at No. 60 Bridge street; about a year later he had added to the business a very much larger stock and the business grew rapidly during the four years. He removed to No. 531 Dutton street six years ago and it became necessary to again to look for more commodious premises, having added a wholesale department and meeting with great success. He still continued to sell the products of his factory in Lowell and surrounding environs and counties.

In 1893, Mr. Hanson secured the sole agency of the celebrated "Fennel Cyrnthians" horse boots for Lowell and vicinity. The cost of these boots are but little over the ordinary goods of this nature, and no doubt Mr. Hanson finds the quality of goods nowadays best sellers, for in all cases quality gives the best satisfaction.

Mr. Hanson's line embraces harness, heavy and light, harness attachments, trimmings, blankets, whips, robes, boots and a complete paraphernalia for the horse.

W. G. EATON, D. V. S.

Veterinary Surgeon.

Comparatively speaking, it may be said that the practice of veterinary medicine and surgery is in its infancy throughout the United States and Canada. A quarter of a century ago there was scarcely a city or town on the American continent that would give adequate support to a veterinary surgeon. Such a state of things cannot now be said to exist, for people have been gradually learning to understand and appreciate the necessity for qualified practitioners in Massachusetts. No protective steps have as yet been taken by the governor as regards the passage of laws favorable to the veterinary profession. In other countries the profession stands upon a firm foundation, and it is safe from quack professors.

W. G. Eaton, Doctor of Veterinary Science, has offices located at C. F. Keyes', stable 32 Church street, Lowell. He was born in Hartford, Conn., 1865, graduated from the Dedham High school, studied human medicine and later gave it up to study veterinary medicine and surgery. Attended colleges in United States and Canada, and graduated from the National Veterinary College, Washington, D. C., with honors. He is inspector of meats and provisions for the town of Dracut, and has filled the same position in various towns and cities of Massachusetts. He has practiced in Lowell for over a year and has a large practice in the city and surrounding towns.

MIDDLESEX STEAM LAUNDRY.

Middlesex St., Corner Eliot.

One of the fast growing achievements in the industrial line of Lowell is that of the Middlesex Steam Laundry, of which F. E. Haines is sole proprietor, and under whose progressive practical business management it is conducted. The Middlesex Steam Laundry is located at 140 Middlesex street. Mr. Haines started to learn the business in 1877 with Isaac E. Scripture, proprietor of the "Old Scripture Laundry" situated on Lawrence street, and in 1883 purchased the old Merrill Steam Laundry located at 18 and 20 Middlesex street. In 1891 he removed to the present location in a two story brick building, 140 Middlesex street, and it is fitted up with all the modern machinery of the day. Mr. Haines employs about 35 to 50 hands with a weekly pay roll of from $250.00 to $350.00. and no doubt turns out more work than any other laundry in the city. His large business has been attained only by strict practical business principles, honest legitimate dealings and personal supervision of every piece of work, whether large or small, before its delivery, and in all cases of delay or of a customer not receiving his articles, immediate notice is requested to be forwarded to Mr. Haines. This leading and finely quartered place has a constant growing business.

LEROY TURNER,

Retail Druggist, 197 Central St.

In no single, modern industry has a business been conducted in such a thorough, practical, business way as that of the drug store located at the corner of Central and Jackson streets, of which the proprietor is Leroy M. Turner.

Mr. Turner is a native of Lowell and was educated in the public schools of the city, beginning his business career 17 years ago. In Oct., 1894, he bought out the store and contents of Ellingwood & Co. at the above location. Mr. Turner is a wide awake, progressive, prominent, fast growing, as well as as successful a merchant as there is in Lowell, and it is the opinion of the public that time will place him in the front rank of the practical enterprises. His location is one of the finest in the city by which all the cars from North Chelmsford, Billerica, Middlesex Village and the Highland district have to pass, giving passengers an opportunity to see the goods all attractively displayed in the windows, with equally attractive prices. This drug store is surely obtaining the esteem of the public in general, for its pre-eminence, the manner in which the business is managed and the prices of goods found at Mr. Turner's store would cause comment in any city outside of the metropolis.

Mr. Turner has one of the finest situations, with handsome interior where electric lights illuminate the store at night and electric fans keep the soda fanciers cool, while attractive cards are displayed throughout the store, which go to show the plain, right to the point sort of character of its management.

LOWELL W. C. T. U.

The "Women's Temperance League" of Lowell was organized in 1875, with 130 members. March 3rd, 1880, the constitution was amended and the name changed to "Woman's Christian Temperance Union," with a membership of 40. In 1892 the membership had increased to 86. For the past two years the membership has increased rapidly to the number of 300; 273 of these are active and 27 are honorary members. Two years and a half ago a reading room was opened in Welle's block and has been kept open every day since except Sundays. A coffee and lunch-table has been added to the room where everyone can be served at all hours.

The W. C. T. U. aims to inculcate temperance principles in the rising generation, believing that a child trained up in the way he should go will not depart from it when he is older. The Loyal Temperance Legion is established to accomplish this object. Children belonging to this organization are required to take the pledge to abstain from the use of wine, beer, cider and all alcoholic liquors as a beverage, also from tobacco and profanity.

The meetings are made interesting with scientific instruction upon the evil effects of the use of all intoxicants, tobacco and opium, and with singing and recitations by the children and pleasant talks upon various topics by competent persons.

The Woman's Christian Temperance Union of Lowell has had under consideration for some time the idea of establishing a coffee house. Coming in contact as they do with the drink problem in its various forms, they have felt assured that if one could be established where men and women could be provided with coffee and lunch at a reasonable price, served in a bright, comfortable room, where reading matter of a wholesome nature could be placed within their reach, it would go far towards counteracting the pernicious effects of the saloon.

Not having available funds to open iust such a place as they desired, and also being unable to find a suitable location at the present time, they have decided to place a coffee and lunch table in their rooms until the way is open for them to establish this much needed work in the city of Lowell. It was decided to commence this work during the convention of the American Missionary Association, which was held in October. They met with great encouragement from the Christians attending the convention.

It is to be commended upon that this admirable society has the co-operation of those who are interested in the uplifting of humanity. Some one has said that "the surest way to reach a poor hungry man is through his stomach." Be that as it may, we know one is always more easily persuaded to do right when they feel warm and comfortable in body. We feel sure that the thoughtful people of Lowell will be glad to assist this organization in its good work.

JOEL KNAPP,

257 Middlesex St.

George L. Richardson started this establishment in 1883, but two years later sold out to Joel Knapp, who is a practical iron worker, having been for 20 years foreman of the Lowell Machine Shops' bolt and nut department, in which responsible position he was succeeded for five years by his son. Joel Knapp's shop is located on the ground floor of Davis & Sargent's block, 257 Middlesex street, occupying two rooms respectively 40 x 90 feet, provided with steam power and containing a complete equipment of machinists' tools and appliances. His working force numbers usually about fifteen, and their output, steadily increasing, aggregated in value for the past year $50,000. This firm manufactures Grosvenor's woodworking machinery and loose pulleys, and builds special machinery of every description to order in superior style, but makes leading specialties of general jobbing, repairing, and manufacturing builders' materials, nuts, washers, cap and set screws, studs, etc., in quantities. Grosvenor's swivel saw-bench, is the latest improvement in this class of devices, adapted to and of capacity for large or small woodworking shops, and complete for splitting, squaring, mitreing and grooving. At the same time it is so constructed as to be instantly changed to saw any mitre or bevel required, lengthwise or crosswise of the wood. They also keep in stock, and supply to order, all kinds of iron-work for the use of builders, such as cast-iron columns and plates, wrought-iron beams, trusses, ties, anchors, bolts, etc., at short notice, and at lowest current prices. They have a large local patronage, but will take pleasure in making estimates and supplying materials, machinery, etc., for shipment to any railroad point.

GEORGE MAKER,

Manufacturer of Picture and Mirror Frames, Corner of John and Merrimack Sts.

One of the most prominent factors of the frame industry in Lowell is the enterprise of George Maker, located in Marble Bank Building, corner of John and Merrimack streets. This house was established in 1891 by

Mr. Maker upon a very small scale and rapidly made its way to the front rank of the trade under the close attention of its manager, and by reason of its honorable, upright business methods. His face was a most familiar one and was always welcome in his numerous former business connections, where his credit and practically unlimited experience have gained him the present prestige he enjoys in his line of business. Today its products are manufactured in enormous quantities and are in active demand for the trade in all parts of the New England states, where they are everywhere recognized as standard in quality, unsurpassed in workmanship, and meet all the requirements of the trade.

His line embraces picture and mirror frames, water colors, etchings, oil paintings, easels and picture supplies. It is the only house in Lowell which carries a reserved stock of French bevel and German plate looking-glasses. These goods can be found in immense quantities in all desired shapes at all times.

Mr. Maker's factory is located at 30 John street. No similar house in the country occupies a more promising position in the industrial line, having the advantage of good facilities, ample resources, experienced management and assistants who help to perfect its growth, and advancement may confidently be predicted to be fully in accord with the past honorable record of usefulness and influence of Mr. Maker's shop.

DAIGNAULT & LAHAISE.

In the Associate Building in the south side corner is situated a neat little barbering establishment, proprietors of which are Daignault & Lahaise, who do a thriving business. They have handsomely arranged parlors with good cabinet filled with French plate mirror, on the second floor, directly over the entrance on Merrimack street. Both proprietors are practical barbers in every sense of the word. In the cut of the Associate building you will notice their sign and individual selves standing in the window.

A visit to these parlors will convince you of their practicability in the barber line, and they will be glad to receive you as a new patron and steady customer.

They are of French descent, of neat appearance and in keeping with their highly recommended hair dressing establishment. They have been established for about a year and the business is constantly growing as a result of their practicability and wide experience who give their close attention to the industry.

FISH & PLUMMER, REAL ESTATE BROKERS.

For the past twenty years this firm has been successfully engaged in an extensive real estate business in Lowell, and their agency rooms 4 and 5 Hamilton block, 137 Central street, opposite the American hotel, is one of the leading enterprises of the kind in the state of Massachusetts. Messrs. Fish & Plummer are experienced real estate agents and have a wide acquaintance in this part of New England, and in fact handle property from all sections of the country. They buy, sell and exchange farms, houses and land, negotiate loans and mortgages, lease tenements and take general supervision of estates, and those contemplating the purchase, sale, or leasing of property would do well to consult this responsible and reliable firm. Reasonable in their commissions and watchful of the interests of their clients, Messrs. Fish & Plummer have firmly established themselves in general confidence, and made their agency the popular medium for those seeking houses or investments, as well as for those desiring to sell or lease reliable tenements or loan on real estate.

Charles T. Fish and John A. Plummer constitute the firm. Mr. Fish served three years in the war of the Rebellion and is quite an earnest worker in the G. A. R. Was on the staff of Past Commander in Chief, John G. B. Q. Adams, and is at present aid-de-camp on staff of Department Commander Joseph W. Thayer.

Mr. Plummer is a very much respected Odd Fellow and belongs to the Merrimack lodge of this city.

JOSIAH GATES & SONS,

Manufacturers of Oak Tan Leather Belting.

A leading house in the Oak Tan Leather Belting in the city of Lowell is Josiah Gates & Sons, who keep an unexcelled line of lace leather, rubber leather, loom strapping, worster apron, rubber belting and mill supplies. This is a prominent house of its line and is located at 307 Market street.

THOMAS M. BOLTON,

Saddlery and Harness Manufacturing.

An enterprise that contributes not a little to the development of the industrial resources of Lowell, and a leading one of its kind, is the establishment of Thomas M. Bolton, Saddlery, Harness and Paraphernalia manufacturer, which was instituted about sixteen years ago at 116 Market street, directly opposite his present number, 311 Market street, where his business has steadily grown. The reputation of his products demanded a more roomy place and today he occupies two spacious places. His sale and harness department at 311 Market street as manufacturer of society paraphernalias is located on Worthen street. He now gives employment to four girls and six men at his factory.

Mr. Bolton is the sole proprietor. He also handles horse furnishings, such as blankets, robes, surcingles, saddlery, etc. He carries an extensive stock of assorted fine whips and everything appertaining to the trade of foreign and domestic goods, and is the only house in Lowell which manufactures a riding saddle.

The advantages this house has to offer are good value at close prices, fine workmanship in harmony with fine quality of stock. Mr. Bolton is a practical harness maker, having learned his trade from his father when a very young man and his experience in fine work for society paraphernalia is gaining for him an increase of trade in that direction.

ELLINGWOOD & CO.,

Corner of Merrimack and Central Sts.

The most famous drug store of the city of Lowell is that of Ellingwood & Co., established in 1870 by C. I. Hood. Mr. Ellingwood took possession in 1885, and it is without doubt the most modern and complete drug store in the city of Lowell. It fronts on both Central and Merrimack streets, with about 120 feet of elegant plate glass. The interior is elegantly decorated with fresco ceiling and quartered oak fixtures. No expense has been spared in furnishing the people of Lowell an "up-to-date" drug store. The location of the drug store is one of the most accessible in the city, having two entrances. The floor of the drug store is inlaid with veneering and steel ceiling of the most artistic design. They have the most expensive and attractive soda fountain without doubt in the New England states, and taking the place all in all it can be said that there is not as pretty and attractive a store in the United States.

Mr. Ellingwood, the proprietor, is determined that nothing but a first class drug store shall be on that corner and he has carried out his views in every particular, in connection with his belief. Members of the firm are energetic and indefatigable in all their efforts to reach the greatest perfection in their accommodations for the trade, and also in the promotion of the substantial welfare and prosperity of the industries of Lowell. They are also manufacturers of Ellingwood's Cough Balsam and make a specialty of prescriptions.

The success of this firm is largely due to its liberal management and honorable dealings, and relations with it will disclose benefits of the most attractive character.

Mr. Ellingwood is a native of Lowell, well known and closely connected with the general welfare of Lowell, and he can be proud of the ownership of the finest equipped drug store in the city of Lowell. This house requires the services of five clerks, of which all but one are registered pharmacists, and they are attentive and extremely polite. An invitation is extended to the public in general to call and inspect the interior of this finely appointed drug store.

SAMUEL BILLINGS,

Livery, Boarding and Feed Stables, 851 Middlesex St.

Mr. Billings started in business about four months ago where he is at present located, and assumed the management of his own stable. He has a most desirable location and commodious premises at the above number, having very convenient carriage sheds and a stable about 60 x 100 feet floor room, with plenty of loft. The floor of the stable is nicely drained and well ventilated, clean and comfortable, containing about 20 stalls, which are utilized solely for stabling horses. Mr. Billings buys only the best hay, straw and grain to feed his horses upon, and parties having their horses lodged at this stable can depend upon them having the best of care and feed. Mr. Billings' assistants are all polite and courteous factors of the stable. Therefore, those wanting a most desirable party, who is an honest dealing man, in possession of their horses, carriages and equipments, will find the above place just to their liking.

Mr. Billings was born in Haydenville, N. B. He is 24 years of age, bright, progressive, wide-awake and enterprising, and gives his personal attention to the management of his stables. The stock is new and clean. His patrons will find him worthy of their esteem.

MYRON BROTHERS,

Shoe Dealers, 400 Merrimack St.

The above heading is the name of three bright shoe dealers who occupy a store opposite the public library. The enterprise of Myron Brothers was established in 1892, and is conducted by three brothers, Andrew, James and John, ages respectfully, 27, 25 and 23. They carry on a thriving shoe business at 400 Merrimack street. Since their beginning they have built up a trade that places them in the front ranks of this line in the city of Lowell. It is a strictly retail house and its trade is annually increasing. The premises occupied by the firm are in the most prominent spot of the city. The three brothers give their business their personal supervisicn. This enterprising firm can confidently be recommended to the public as being strictly reliable in the representation of all goods sold by them, which meet the approval of the most discriminating taste in the shoe line.

G. C. PRINCE & SON,

Stationery, Art and Literature.

Lowell enjoys the proud pre-eminence of being able to say that it has one of the finest stationery, book, art and literature stores in the state, that of G. C. Prince & Son, 108 Merrimack street, it being probably one of the best known houses in the city of Lowell in its line. Mr. Prince commenced business in Lawrence thirty years ago and conducted the same for seven years upon Main st., of that place. For 23 years he has been an established merchant of this community, of no little importance, and has always been general agent for leading Boston and New York daily papers. Stationery of every description, books and fine literature, frames, pictures, all can be found at this establishment.

Both Mr. Prince and his son are men of remarkable energy, and their success has been marked by integrity of character and noble principle. For over thirty years this house has been well known throughout the community and adjoining counties as being the leading representative firm in its line. They have lately moved from the corner of Prescott and Merrimack streets to a handsome site which is situated at 108 Merrimack street.

The firm are the most extensive dealers in their line of this section and the stock handled embraces everything which is in harmony with stationery. This house is thoroughly identified with the development of Lowell in conducting the largest enterprise of its kind in the city. This firm may be justly named as one of the foremost factors of Lowell's trade resources.

Barristers Hall.

T. D. HARTFORD,

Clothing, Hat and Gents' Furnishings, Central St., Near Merrimack.

This enterprise was established in 1890 by Mr. Hartford, who has been a resident of Lowell for the past 20 years, and therefore is one of the prominent representatives of this important department of commerce.

The building occupied by Mr. Hartford affords about 35 x 70 feet floor room, which is lit by four arc lights, that give his display windows an elegant appearance in the evening. From the inception of the business, the policy of the management has always been directed toward providing the most advanced facilities for the sale of his line, and it now enjoys an unsurpassed amount of the trade in Lowell, which is constantly increasing day by day, and the people have learned to place great confidence in the representation of anything known to come from Mr. Hartford's establishment. The business is conducted under experienced and progressive management. This house will be found equal to all the requirements of customers in its line, the most liberal and fair dealing methods prevailing.

THE MacDONALD GYMNASIUM

For Massage, Swedish Movement Cure, Turkish, Russian, or Tub Baths.

The interest of physicians in the value of baths in many diseased conditions is increasing, and confidence in these special baths has come with reports from bathers of the supervision and care given. Those who have never taken a Turkish bath would be surprised to know how refreshing they are.

Have you ever taken a Turkish bath? If not, there is a great delight in store for you. It is often considered a luxury, but by those who frequent baths, it is esteemed almost a necessity. It is a panacea for many ills, and a delightful remedy to take. If you feel the symptoms of a cold upon you, it is the part of wisdom to hasten to the bath. Very many have thus escaped long struggles with colds through the efficacy of the bath as a restorative. A Turkish bath is not, as most people imagine, always given in the same way. There are many variations. In these baths, each bather is carefully watched and advised as to the best bath for his or her individual need. A fine massage is given here, and a wet massage, which is most invigorating and refreshing, and very effective in all stomach and bowel difficulties, and all cases of inflammation and heat. A course of baths, with or without massage, is the surest relief from the pains left by La Grippe.

WATER AND MASSAGE CURE.

We are ready to give Massage treatment at the Baths at any time during the day. A Water Cure department has been opened, under experienced and competent supervision. The Water Massage here used is very agreeable, especially when the skin is sensitive or there is internal heat or external irritation. We are prepared to give Water Treatments, Sitz Baths, Half Baths, etc., at Odd Fellows' building, Middlesex street, Lowell, Mass.

Lowell Northern Depot.

The Gymnasium Baths are under the general supervision of Miss MacDonald, who may be seen in the gymnasium during her office hours, by patients sent by physicians, who may need special care. Bathers are not rushed through, as in many baths, but each one receives the bath best suited to her needs. First baths are carefully watched and the timid and nervous reassured.

GEORGE E. KIRBY,

Cor. Powell and Chelmsford Sts.

One of the factors of the city of Lowell is George E. Kirby's paint store, which is a rare feature in this section of the city. Although it has been established but a short time it is gaining ground very fast. Mr. Kirby runs in connection with his paint store, house painting, graining, kalsomining, and gives his personal attention to all the work, and free estimates on both large and small orders. He is widely known in that section of the city as a man of wide experience, and it can be said that he can be thoroughly relied upon in the discharge of every duty.

He is 36 years of age and has resided in Lowell 33 years. The locality in which his store is situated is thickly settled, and a store of that kind has been greatly needed in the past, and we are pleased to say that Mr. Kirby will in the future be on hand to contract for anything in his line of business, at the most reasonable prices. He has at present nine skilled workmen to whom he gives employment. At times he employs as many as fifteen. The store and work department have his personal attention and he gives ample guarantee that nothing but satisfactory work can be the outcome of his labor. Paints, brushes, kalsomine, paris green, everything appertaining to the paint line is carried in large quantities at Mr. Kirby's place.

Special attention is called to interior work of which he makes a specialty.

JOHN THOMPSON,

Merchant Tailor, 189 Middlesex St.

A new merchant tailoring establishment was opened at No. 189 Middlesex street, Feb. 1st., 1895, by J. T. Thompson who has had an experience of twenty-five years in the business. He has a very neat, tidy place to show customers his unmade materials. The trade of Mr. Thompson embraces every style, kind and quality of merchant tailoring. Satisfaction is surely guaranteed in every case. The house proposes to extend its trade by offering a cordial invitation to the public to inspect it, and it has already received marked attention from buyers. The enterprise is sure of success as its manager gives his personal attention to the making department, which with his wide experience, he dictates and oversees all details, which gives evidence of future progression in establishing a larger business.

BIRTHPLACE OF GEORGE E. MITCHELL,

Kennebunk, York Co., Me.

Born Aug. 25, 1837.

On April 16th, 1879, one of the finest days that ever shone on earth, 1,560 beings, myself and Mrs. Mitchell included, left the port of San Francisco, Cal., for Portland, Oregon, on the steamship Great Republic, second largest in the world. April 22d, between eleven and one o'clock P. M., we ran ashore on Sand Island. April 23d, we were all saved in life boats but 13, amid the most terrific thunder, lightning and rain storm ever any human being experienced, and long to be remembered by the passengers. That day will never be forgotten by any soul who was on that ship. The law only allowed her to carry 900 passengers; still she had 1,560. All the inhabitants of the Pacific Slope will remember this incident. This picture was taken by "Tabor," of San Francisco, the next day after I landed back at that port.

No. 1.

MITCHELL'S ORIGINAL KIDNEY PLASTERS

Absorb all diseases of the KIDNEYS and restore them to a healthy condition. Old chronic Kidney sufferers say they received no relief until they tried *Mitchell's Kidney Plasters.*

Cheap articles are dear at any price. When a person offers real, genuine gold dollars for fifty cents, beware! something must be wrong. Same with **KIDNEY PLASTERS.** When unscrupulous druggists offer you others in place of *Mitchell's* and say they are just as good, even superior, and larger, at half the price, beware! something must be wrong. Get *Mitchell's*, and take no others, if you want a SURE CURE. Sold by all druggists and dealers in medicines everywhere, or sent by mail on receipt of Fifty Cents. Manufactured by the Novelty Plaster Works, Lowell, Mass., U. S. A. G. E. Mitchell, Founder and Sole Proprietor. Founded in 1864.

No. 2.

MITCHELL'S ORIGINAL RHEUMATIC PLASTERS

For the cure of Rheumatism and Gout. "Whew! Dis de chap stole my onions; smell him breaf!" For you, old, rich, lazy, guzzling beer drinkers, who have more money than brains, and do nothing but drink, eat, sleep and be merry, until you get so fat and corpulent that you can't see your own feet, who toddle backward and forward from one grog shop to another, drinking beer and other intoxicating drinks; when you have a bad spell of Gout or Rheumatism, just tackle a *Mitchell's* **RHEUMATIC PLASTER**, the pioneer of plaster fame; and if the Plaster don't get the best of your aches and pains, then I miss my guess, and you will say another sinner is converted and another soul made happy by the use of *Mitchell's Original Rheumatic Plaster*, ingredients of which are composed of rare medicinal gums, only found in *Mitchell's*, that cure like the touch of the magic wand. Other makers copy *Mitchell's* in size and shape, which any fool could do, but in the absence of *Mitchell's* compound, which is peculiar to itself, you might as well use molasses or sticky fly paper and expect it to cure. Manufactured by the NOVELTY PLASTER WORKS, Lowell, Mass.; G. E. Mitchell, Founder and Sole Proprietor. Founded in 1864. The Pioneer of Plaster fame. Sold by all dealers in medicine, or mailed from the works on receipt of 25 cents.

No. 3. MITCHELL'S ORIGINAL

PERFORATED BELLADONNA PLASTERS,

Especially adapted for complaints of ladies; superior to all other Belladonna Plasters known. The most scientific known to the science of man. As Morse caught the lightning and caused it to talk, so did *Mitchell* conceive the idea of combining Belladonna with rubber and causing a cure. If you desire a **BELLADONNA PLASTER** which can be relied upon at all times, under all circumstances, the most scientific known to the science of man, ask for MITCHELL'S and take no other, and be sure his picture, taken in 1864, is printed on the Plaster and circular, as all others are base imitations.

No. 4. MITCHELL'S ORIGINAL

CURE-ALL CORN AND BUNION PLASTERS.

Last but Not Least.

Nine cases out of ten where *Mitchell's Cure-All* **Corn and Bunion Plaster** is applied, the pain leaves at once. This Plaster is just as good for callous Feet and for all Sores on the Feet usually caused by chafing. If it pains you after wearing a while, remove, and in a day or two apply a fresh piece. For Corns and Bunions and Soft Corns:— Cover the Corn or Bunion all over with a Plaster, and a sure cure will be effected. Persons who will wear tight boots and shoes to make their feet look small, should always use *Mitchell's Cure-All* **CORN AND BUNION PLASTERS.** They are as thin as a sheet of paper, and do not take up so much room, and are not as clumsy as the old felt corn and bunion plasters. *One trial will make a cripple dance for joy.* Ask for **Mitchell's Cure-All Corn and Bunion Plaster.** Sold by Druggists and dealers in medicine everywhere; 12 sheets in each box. Price 50 cents per Box.

NOVELTY PLASTER WORKS,

Lowell, Mass.

Mr. G. E. Mitchell is sole proprietor and founder of the Novelty Plaster works. This business was established in 1864 and is without doubt the pioneer of all kinds of plasters. He has a finely located factory directly opposite the Court house, situated on Elm street, having a complete floorage of abut 65,000 quare feet. The building is a four story structure with all the modern machinery and improvements, for the plaster business, with printing, labeling, shipping and receiving departments.

The finishing room on the upper story is acknowledged by all who visit the works to be the most pleasant work room in the city of Lowell, commanding a grand view overlooking the city.

This establishment is growing so rapidly that since their foundation they have added a number of rooms, and at present are very crowded in their quarters. The building is heated by steam with every department complete in its respective detail.

Mr. Mitchell is a native ot Kennebunk, York County, Maine, and his enterprise is acknowledged by all who know him, or of him, as having leading plaster works of this country. The high reputation obtained for the products of the house has been fully maintained under Mr. Mitchell's personal management, and his ability and capacity have been tested by the continual success of his enterprise, which enjoys a prominence in the field of industry only accorded to such establishments as have been conducted on the enduring principles of originality and conception of perfection in all products.

--- --- ---

E. W. YOUNG,

Room 67 Hildreth Building, Barber and Ladies' Hair Dresser.

One of the leading, if not the oldest hair dressing establishment in the city of Lowell, is that of E. W. Young, located in the Hildreth building, rooms 8 and 9. Mr. Young is a native of the city of Lowell and began business in a small way in the old Museum Building about seventeen years ago, and eleven years ago moved to his present quarters in the above building, at which time he connected with his business a ladies' hair dressing department, which has been a continued success ever since its birth. His rooms cover a floorage of about 40 feet square and the walls are handsomely decorated with mirrors and mechanical appliances used in the operation of his business. Mr. Young brings direct experience to bear on the management of the business and possesses an intimate knowledge of the details of the barber business as well as the requirements of customers.

The premises occnpied are really too small for the rapidly growing business. He has at present eight chairs, three of which are for ladies. This department is separated from the gent's department, having lady attendants who are skilled in their trade and who are posted from week to week in the New York society of fashion, of which Mr. Young is a member. The elevator furnishes close connections, his establishment being the first door to the left from the elevator exit. Mr. Young is not only a practical barber but also the manufacturer of Young's French Lustre, Arbut's Curling Fluid and French Dressing for the hair. He is the first one who has learned the art of bleaching and dying perfectly, a matter which but few barbers are posted in.

MISS ROSE DECOMBE,

Principal Lowell School of Shorthand and Typewriting.

The secluded little village of Howick, in the Province of Quebec, was where Miss Decombe first saw the light of day, Aug. 10, 1868. She was the only daughter of Joseph Decombe, a prominent business man, who kept a large tannery, on the outskirts of the town. During the first years of her scholastic life, she attended the common schools of her native village and then was sent to the St. Hilaire Academy at St. Chrysostome. Having gone through the courses of that institution, she entered, as a boarder, a convent, conducted by the Sisters of the Holy Name of Jesus and Mary, of St. Alouysius, P. Q., and remaining there for three years, graduated with high rank in 1885.

The three years following were spent in the quiet of her own home, devoting the entire time to the study of music, under a private teacher from Montreal. But Miss Decombe, desiring to put to good advantage the thorough education which had been bestowed upon her, finally decided to accept a position which had been offered to her, by the British American Dyeing Co., at their head office in Montreal, and for two years acted as clerk and book-keeper in that establishment.

While acting in that capacity, she became aware of the value of stenography, and conceived the idea of coming to the United States in order to receive a thorough course in that useful branch. So in 1890, bidding farewell to Canada, Miss Decombe came to Boston and entered the Boston School of Shorthand and Typewriting. After a year's unceasing study, she finished, and became assistant teacher in that well known school.

Being well versed in the arts and mysteries of shorthand and typewriting, Miss Decombe felt herself competent of undertaking the charge of a school in the above branches, so in 1891 selected Lowell as her field of labor. Visiting several business blocks, it finally became her decision to locate in Central Block. A small room on the second floor was chosen, but so rapid was the success of her enterprise that it was necessary to secure the two large adjoining rooms.

Miss Decombe's school has already acquired the reputation of being the best of its kind in Lowell and vicinity, as the many young ladies and young gentlemen filling important positions in the principal offices of this city and outside fully attest.

Miss Decombe is a bright and energetic lady, well qualified in her profession, as the success of her work has shown.

D. H. NICKERSON & CO.,

Tailors, Fiske Block, Central St.

The firm of D. H. Nickerson & Co., tailors, who occupy the pleasant and commodious chambers, 2 and 3 Fiske block 219 Central street was established Oct. 8, '94.

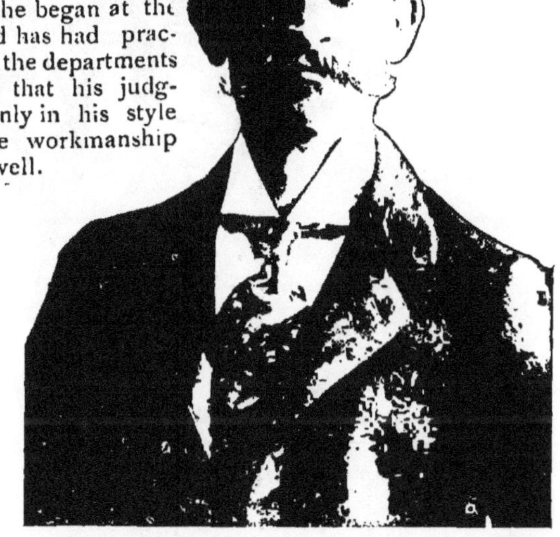

Before coming to Lowell, Mr. Nickerson, for ten years, was connected with the leading tailoring houses in Boston, and his experience there. with the best class of trade, estab lished for him his present excellen standing. As a boy, he began at the foot of the ladder, and has had practical experience in all the departments of a tailor's trade, so that his judgment is efficient not only in his style and goods, but in the workmanship and minor details as well.

Many people in Lowell, the younger men especially, think that it is necessary to go to Boston for their tailoring. They think the styles are newer, the goods are finer, the cutting better. This is not so; and it is just this class of men that Mr. Nickerson particularly invites to inspect his stock. His idea is to supply only the best of work to Lowell people, and show them how entirely un-

Highland Club House.

necessary it is to buy out of town, when the latest styles and goods can be had at home.

Mr. Nickerson is also a competent ladies' tailor, making a specialty of jackets, capes, etc., and is well posted in the latest New York and Paris styles.

As a guarantee of their ability to do first class work, they do not advise a customer to take any garment unless perfectly satisfactory in every way.

LOWELL RENDERING COMPANY.

The Lowell Rendering Company is one of the great factors of the industries of the city of Lowell. It is engaged in handling general rendering materials and has bought a large lot of land in South Lowell, just below the U. S. Cartridge company's land, which lies between the Boston & Maine Railroad and the Concord River. It is their intention to make this establishment one of the largest of its kind in the state, doing a general rendering and soap manufacturing business. They will build larger works at their present location, where the work of manufacturing soap, etc., will be conducted.

Mr. D. Whithed is general manager and treasurer. This concern is not a very old one, having only been established since November 1st, 1894, but its immense growth has been so rapid that the present quarters at No. 429 School street, are far too small for them. The work upon the new building will no doubt be completed in the near future. At present they run twelve wagons for the collection and delivery of the manufactured product.

Mr. Whithed is among the most progressive and substantial business men of Lowell, and is largely interested in every important enterprise. The company has always been subject to all developments and the welfare of Lowell by conducting the affairs of their house with judgment and vigor. They have advanced the interest of their customers in every legitimate manner and at the same time developed a business that is alike creditable to this community and to themselves.

LOWELL CHIROPODICAL, MANICURE AND HAIR PARLORS.

Lowell is in possession of a Chiropodical, Manicure and Hair Dressing Parlor. It can be said that Dr. Judkins and Dr. Howe, the proprietors of the above institution have done business in the O'Donnell & Gilbride building for the past year in a very successful manner. It is the only one of its kind in the city where they combine facial massage and remove warts and blemishes of the face and hands.

The methods employed are all of a scientific nature and will surely give satisfaction to patrons calling upon them for the above purposes. They are becoming widely known every day as thoroughly responsible and as having a wide experience in the above line.

All are invited to call and inspect the treatment, and ladies are especially invited to inspect the hair dressing department, which is conducted by experienced hair dressers of wide reputation. Any information required will be answered by mail.

Wm. T. TRUE.

Wm. T. True, is the name of one of the leading contractors of Lowell, whose experience dates back to boyhood. The past four years he has conducted a business in Lowell, putting up a number of fine buildings, one of which is the well known Gee Machine shop on Fletcher street. Mr. True was employed some four years ago by the popular firm of Norcross Bros., of Worcester, who built the Ames building of Boston, the largest building in that city today. By natural instinct Mr. True is a carpenter, builder, and contractor; he is a native of Lowell.

The wide experience he has obtained places him in a position to contract and build anything, no matter how large or small; he employs from time to time 25 to 50 men, all of whom are skilled in their various lines of trade.

Mr. True has gained a reputation for putting up a building in less time than any other contractor in a satisfactory manner, containing nothing but first class workmanship. Honorable dealing has been one of the features of dealings with Mr. True, which has surely added to the immense increase in his business, and all who have future business relations with him will likewise be treated.

Mr. True completed a handsome residence at 45 to 53 Moore street in the spring of '95, which has attracted considerable notice; it occupies a most prominent location just off Gorham street, the cut of which is on opposite page. Mr. True is also agent for the Brattleboro Clothes Dryer Company in Lowell, which is said to be the best article of its kind upon the market.

O'DONNELL & GILBRIDE,

Corner of Palmer and Merrimack Sts.

This old establishment and leading enterprise was originally founded in 1880 in a small store on Merrimack street occupying a floorage of about 20 x 80 feet. Three years later the business grew so rapidly that they added about the same amount of floorage and doubled the stock of dry and fancy goods. In 1886 there became another necessity for enlargement and they removed their store and leased with it more commodious apartments of about the same size. In 1888 there became still another pressing necessity for space, the growth being so tremendously rapid that they leased the building in the rear and built a bridge connecting the two. In 1891 they built the handsome building which is located on Palmer street. The floorage they occupy is no less than an acre and a half, and of late years they have added a carpet and furniture department, making a store second to none in the city of Lowell, and it can be said that it is the oldest store handling the number of departments which O'Donnell & Gilbride display. The store is most attractively situated and is managed very conservatively. It would take a large space to describe every detail in connection with this concern as it has a history of sufficient time, growth, attractiveness and outlook of possibilities which would be impossible to mention in this book, but it can be said that this concern has made its reputation by honorable dealing and furnishing goods to the public at prices in harmony with quality, handling goods only direct from the manufacturers which enables them to keep up the pace with prices of the metropolis.

P. J. BURLEIGH,

Cigar Manufacturer, Associate Building.

This house was founded by Mr. Burleigh March 1, 1895, and has steadily grown since that date, so that at the present time he requires a number of assistants in the manufacture of the widely known cigar "80-7," ten cent cigar which is making a reputation for Mr. Burleigh very rapidly. Mr. Burleigh is also the leader of the National Band of Lowell.

The premises occupied for the business are located in the Associate Building on the second fioor. which comprise commodious rooms for the manufacture of cigars. The above brand will meet the approval of the most fastidious taste. Each cigar is the product of the labor of one person and it can be thoroughly relied upon in uniformity, material and workmanship. Mr. Burleigh gives the business his personal supervision. This enterprise gives ample evidence of stability and pre-eminence and any relations with it will disclose many advantages not easily duplicated in this market.

GEORGE Le BANC,

19 East Merrimack St.

Mr. Le Banc is the name of the proprietor of the East Merrimack Street Bakery which is located three doors from the bridge. The proprietor of this establishment is but 24 years of age, but he is an "up-to-date" hustler.

The business was established last March, and since it has been increasing gradually through the clear and conservative business management of Mr. Le Banc. In the busy season Mr. Le Banc gives positions to three bakers and runs one team.

He served his apprenticeship with F. M. Mills and W. Nichols & Co., of this city, as a manufacturing baker. His line embraces home made Vienna cream breads, cakes, pies, and he makes a specialty of fancy wedding cakes. The building which he occupies is in a good location and very neatly kept, having the most recent methods of making, baking and moulding of fancy pastries, etc.

W. E. WOODSIDE,

Photographer, Five Cent Saving Bank Building.

Mr. Woodside is a photographer of fourteen years experience and one of the oldest, highly reputed photographers in the city of Lowell. This house was established in 1886, July 9, and since that time has done a successful and satisfactory photographic business.

Mr. Woodside is a man of wide reputation in his line of business and consequently his product is in keeping with fine work. It is safe to say that no photographer in Lowell surpasses the work turned out by this well known house. Mr. Woodside gives the business his personal attention, guarantees his work and prices are always in harmony with quality. Mr. Woodside is a liberal, public minded, business man and conducts his business in a thoroughly practical, business way. He has gained many friends in this city in his nine years of location and he will be pleased to establish an acquaintance with any and all who require first-class photographic work at reasonable prices. Such are given a special invitation to call and have a trial sitting for a trial order.

Mr. Woodside's establishment is one of the many factors in the city. He has a prominent location on the main thoroughfare, and all who do business with him will find him honorable in all details of such transactions.

H. E. HARRIS,

Jewelry and Literature, 10 Appleton St.

The progressive establishment of H. E. Harris, located at No. 10 Appleton street, was established in 1892 in a new wooden structure at the corner of Appleton and Central streets. Mr. Harris started in a small way in 1892, but has constantly added small departments to his place at the above number, until now he runs two branches of business with the jewelry, jewelry repairing, broker business, literature and news rooms.

Mr. Harris is a thorough business man and the prediction of his future growth is sure to come to pass. He makes a specialty of literature, books, stationery, and is agent for the metropolis editions of not a few. Mr. Harris has a very fine location and a separate display window for both jewelry and his news department which gives employment to from three to five hands. While the trade of the house is largely local, its news customers are found in all parts of the environs and the local public is also interested in loans, etc. Mr. Harris conducts the business under his personal supervision and is an enterprising and esteemed citizen and extremely accommodating.

F. G. MITCHELL,

Founder and Proprietor of the Bon Marche.

Born in Lowell in 1853, he is still a young man, his present age being but 38. He acquired his education in the public schools of his native city like hundreds of other young lads.

His father decided that he should become a pattern maker. At the age of 16 went to work at 90 cents a day and was told after working there a short time that he must improve or get out. Never despairing, he sought and obtained a position with A. C. Skinner, who kept a dry goods store on Merrimack street, and from him obtained his first knowledge of the dry and fancy goods business. After having been there three days Mr. Skinner called on his mother and told her that her son was not adapted to the dry goods trade and wished her to tell him, and furthermore to keep him at home as he had no further use for him. But as a boy of determined spirit he lost no time in asserting himself, and said, "I will not leave, and I will learn the business." With this decision he went back to the store and began to work with such vim that no explanation was asked regarding his appearance at the store. Mr. Skinner told him if he kept on improving as he had done he would suit him all right, and here he started for years of toil, sweeping floors, washing windows, carrying parcels, and selling dry goods, etc., at the same time grasping every particle of knowledge and value he could get.

Mr. Mitchell in his younger days went to California, bought a ranch and with saving during these five years he returned with $500. and made his first bid for the patronage of the people, taking a store on Merrimack street. After six years in his original store Mr. Mitchell bought out Miss Hamblett, who for years had conducted a millinery business at the corner of Merrimack and Kirk streets. A year later Mr. Mitchell bought out in special connection with his brother, C. Mitchell, a boot and shoe store and here a partnership was continued a couple of years. when Mr.

Bon Marche Building.

F. G. Mitchell retired from this branch in favor of his brother, Charles A. Mitchell. About six months after opening the store Mr. Mitchell obtained the lease of several pieces of property, on which stood eight millinery stores, a hotel, two barns, a wood yard, a public laundry. a doctor's cottage, as well as considerable vacant land. and began remodeling the Lovejoy property and building the Kirk street building. Two years later a four story addition was erected in the rear of five millinery stores on Merrimack street, and two years later was begun the erection of the recent addition. This comprises his present store and contains 60,-000 feet.

ALLAN FRASER,

Gents' Furnishing Goods, Odd Fellows' Block, Middlesex St.

The store of Allan Fraser is pleasantly situated in the new Odd Fellows' Building, 90 Middlesex street, where is kept a full and first class line of gent's furnishings. Mr. Fraser came from the northern part of New York in the year of 1889 and started out to do battle for himself in Lowell.

He secured employment from A. C. Stevens, the wholesale and retail druggist and fancy goods dealer, where he remained for three years, when his employer decided to sell out. He then decided to enter business on his own responsibility, bought out his employer, and for a time located at 105 Middlesex street, but finding the place too small, he removed to his present quarters, where he is conducting a thriving business, which embraces everything in gent's furnishings: white shirts, collars and cuffs, underwear, hosiery, novelties in neckwear, hats and caps of the latest design. This house is the standard for square dealings; everything is made satisfactory or money refunded, at the store of Allan Fraser.

CHRIS HOLMES,

Suits, Ladies' Skirts, Wraps, Cloaks and Jackets.

The above enterprise is the only representative, new and important house in the city of Lowell which occupies a prominent location on Merrimack street, where it has great facilities of displaying the stylish, neat, attractive, "up-to-date" ladies' wearing apparel which can always be found at this house, and without a doubt it can be said that this live house is the leading one of its kind in the city of Lowell.

His line embraces ladies' jackets, duck suits, laundered waists, silk waists, summer wash suits, wrappers, jackets, etc., and everything identified with ladies' wearing apparel. The house gives employment to about twelve skilled sales ladies in the busy season.

Mr. Holmes is an expert judge in buying the above lines of goods, and his resources for obtaining goods directly from the manufacturers give him the best opportunity to produce material, quality, skilled workmanship, and prices in keeping with the same. Mr. Holmes is an enterprising man who is closely connected with the growth and advancement of Lowell; he is also highly esteemed by the community for his liberal

TRADERS NATIONAL BANK

business policy, and he justly invites the influential patronage secured by his energy and enterprise. The house has a liberal patronage and is truly a popular one under such conservative management; it also commends itself as one that may be emphatically relied upon to furnish only such garments as shall be first class in every respect.

THE TRADERS NATIONAL BANK,

Nos. 8 and 10 Middlesex St.

Capital, - - - - - $200,000.

Chas. J. Glidden, president; Eugene S. Hylan, vice-president; Wm. F. Hills, cashier; Charles A. Grant, notary public; Frederic A. Holden, teller; Amos. F. Hill, assistant teller; Martin M. Glidden, clerk, Clinton, R., Carpenter and book-keeper. Banking hours, 8 a. m. to 4 p. m. Saturday 8 a. m. to 1 p. m. Discount daily.

DIRECTORS.

John C. Burke,	William F. Mills,	Michael Corbett,
Eugene S. Hylan,	Solomon K. Dexter,	James H. Mills,
Chas. J. Glidden,	Asa C. Russell,	Othello O. Greewood,
Robert Simpson,	Jesse N. Trull.	

SAVINGS DEPARTMENT.

Open same hours as above, and Saturday evenings from 7 to 9. Money deposited the first three days of any month will draw interest from the first day at the rate of 4 per cent. per annum, compounding twice each year. The amount of money that any person may deposit is not limited except by special action of the directors. For rules and regulations see pass book.

Safety deposit boxes for rent, $5 to $25 per annum, according to size. W. F. Hills and Charles Grant, commissioners to qualify civil officers. Connected with long distance telephone.

APPLETON NATIONAL BANK,

No. 6 Appleton Block, Central St.

Capital, - - - - - $300,000.

J. F. Kimball, president; E. K. Perley, cashier; Fred H. Ela, teller; George E. King, M. T. Pierce, Fred N. Morse, clerks.

DIRECTORS.

H. H. Wilder,	Wm. E. Livingston,	J. W. C. Pickering
J. F. Kimball,	Fred A. Buttrick,	Geo. W. Fifield,
Addison Putnam,	Geo. O. Whiting,	Henry M. Knowles.

Annual meetings, second Tuesday in January; dividends, first Monday in January, April, July and October; discount, Mondays and Thursdays.

Dividends payable in Boston, collected without charge.

THE PRESCOTT NATIONAL BANK,

20 Central St.

Incorporated 1850. Re-organized 1865.
Capital, - - - - - $300,000.

Hapgood Wright, president; Alonzo A. Coburn, vice-president; Fred Blanchard, cashier; clerks, Geo. R. Chandler, E. E. Sawyer, Mark A. Adams, Herbert Burrage.

DIRECTORS.

Geo. F. Richardson,	Daniel Gage,	Alonzo A. Coburn,
Hapgood Wright,	Charles A. Stott,	J. W. Abbott,
Charles H. Coburn,	W. A. Ingham,	J. A. Bartlett.

Annual meetings, second Tuesday in January; discount days, Mondays and Thursdays; dividends payable first of April and October. Bank hours, 8 to 4. Closed Saturdays at 1 P. M.

BARRISTERS HALL.

Barristers Hall was formerly a Methodist church, and away back in 1830 Dr. J. C. Ayer bought the place and in 1861 it was renovated and remodeled into private offices. The first floor always having been used for stores, which are now occupied by Ellingwood, the well known druggist, T. D. Hartford, one of Lowell's clothiers, next door to which is A. M. Huntoon's shoe store and between which is located E. A. Burgess, who conducts a news and periodical store.

William H. Anderson, attorney-at-law, is the present owner of the building, since May, 1893. The top floor is occupied by the well-known photographer, J. S. Marion, and the Zimmer Orchestra which is gaining a reputation in the furnishing of music at reasonable prices to all who are in want of the same. The following are occupants of the above building:

Wm. H. Anderson, attorney; C. H. McIntire, attorney; D. R. Wallace, insurance; Francis W. Qua, attorney; Fred P. Marble, attorney; Jos. F. Lapierre, constable; John J. Pickman, attorney; John J. Harvey, attorney; John L. Hunt, attorney; John P. Searle, constable; John B. Swift, broker and insurance attorney; Henry G. Cushing, sheriff; Philip J. Farley, attorney; Geo. F. Stiles, sheriff; Alvah S. Baker, sheriff; Samuel B. Wyman, attorney, Geo. H. Stevens, attorney.

ARTHUR H. SLATER,

Flat Iron Building, Corner Westford and Pine Sts.

A leading and prominent representative of the retail grocery trade is that of the house of Arthur H. Slater. The business was originally established by his father some years ago, and after having conducted it under his name for a number of years, his son become identified with the concern, and about a year and a half ago purchased the entire interest, since which time the career of the house has steadily advanced and a large and increasing trade has been the result. The premises occupied for the business are located at the junction of Westford and Pine streets, with a frontage on each, which makes it the most complete grocery store in the city with its accommodations for entrance and nicely arranged interior, which is adorned with the luxuries of life, comprising everything in the grocery line. He makes specialties of flour, teas, syrups, molasses, etc., which are procured from first-class resources and offered to the trade at the lowest prices consistent with quality.

In all departments of the business advanced methods prevail and the most complete facilities are placed at the disposal of customers, having telephone connections, efficient clerks, delivery and order wagons, and satisfaction is guaranteed in dealing with such an esteemed house.

SPENCER, ARTIST AND SIGN PAINTER,

22 Middle St.

The only painters in the city who do anything in sign work and gilding, is the well known firm of Spencer & Co., which is located at No. 22 Middle street. Mr. Spencer has a practical experience in the business of over twenty years, having worked for the largest painting establishment in Boston, which turned out only first class work. He is a native of Cambridge, Mass., and in 1882 became identified with Lowell's business men in the above industry. He gives employment to five skilled hands, who do artistic sign work such as show cards, gilding glass, window work, brass work, etc. This house does nothing but first class work, and wherever his work is seen there can be noticed inscribed in small letters, "Spencer." Mr. Spencer is closely identified with the business growth of Lowell and has built for himself a reputation which is creditable to the city, as well as to himself. All relations with this firm will be found of the most agreeable nature, and prices are always in harmony with first class work.

T. C. ENTWISTLE,

104 Worthen St.

One of the most prominent manufacturers of balling, linking or chaining warps of every description, is T. C. Entwistle, who is the largest manufacturer of the kind in the New England states. He also manufactures all kinds of rebeaming, dye tubes and card grinding machines which are a specialty. This house has grown from small beginnings, until at present it occupies a factory running from Worthen to Dutton streets. employing a large number of hands, all of whom are skilled in their line of business.

Mr. Entwistle is closely identified with the industrial progress of the city of Lowell, also to all commercial interests. A large proportion of his trade extends throughout the New England States both south and west. The shop is equipped with the most modern facilities for the manufacture of his line, and his establishment is large and spacious. Mr. Entwistle is one of Lowell's public spirited men and he has been a great factor in the industrial line for the past 20 years. The business done by him has only been accomplished through profitable dealings.

LOWELL BOARD OF TRADE.

This body is an incorporated organization composed of some 350 merchants, manufacturers and other leading citizens, who are associated to promote the material progress of the city ot Lowell. The board has widely advertised the advantages of the city for manufacturing, in the way of freight facilities (Boston rates) and labor.

It is unquestionably due to able and conservative management and to the steadiness, skill and intelligence of the labor element, that all industries planted at Lowell thrive, and that although production, was curtailed and some stoppages occurred during the recent business depression, no wrecks were left behind and no labor disturbances of importance resulted therefrom.

The manufacturers of Lowell are now (July, 1895) fully employed, and a period of extension of plants has already set in. A feature of the industrial system at Lowell is the low cost of a comfortable living, due to a policy adopted over seventy years ago, known as the "Lowell Plan."

The officers of the board for 1895 are George A. Hanscom, president, James T. Smith, secretary, G. W. Knowlton, treasurer, with 25 directors. Regular meetings are held at the rooms in Central Block on the second Tuesday evening of each month, except in July and August.

Full data as to sites for manufacturing, rent, or cost of floor space, water, light, heat, power, labor, etc., are furnished by the secretary on application. Telephone, 80.

CENTRAL BLOCK.

The Central Block is one of the finest buildings in the city of Lowell, the most convenient and in the most desirable location, containing only first class tenants from top to bottom. It is a five-story brick structure (a cut of which is to be found in this book) with two elevators, driven by hydraulic power and lighted by electricity. The building is equipped throughout with the Cutler Mailing Chutes and delivering system, and has electric bells and speaking tube connections with all the rooms.

The ground floor is occupied by J. L. Chalifoux, clothier, shoer, gent's furnisher and complete outfitter. At the corner of the block is situated Durant & Rogers' well-known jewelry store, which is, without doubt, the finest site for a jewelry establishment in the city of Lowell? As you ascend the staircase the first sign that meets your eye is that of Steve Laughton, who is a practical barber in every sense of the word. As you walk down the hall to the left Dr. E. Holt's office comes in view, he occupying room 16. Directly opposite is located Dr. Sargent's office at 27, he being a well known physician. At the front of the staircase facing the two above offices is the Traders & Mechanics Insurance Company, who occupy rooms 26, 28 and 29. As you go down the corridor, the next sign is that of Dr. Chadbourne, who occupies rooms 22 and 23. Opposite that is the office of J. H. Guillett, attorney-at-law, whose numbers are 18 and 19. Meeting in the center once more, where the elevators are located, is the office of the well-known G. W. Batchelder, attorney-at-law

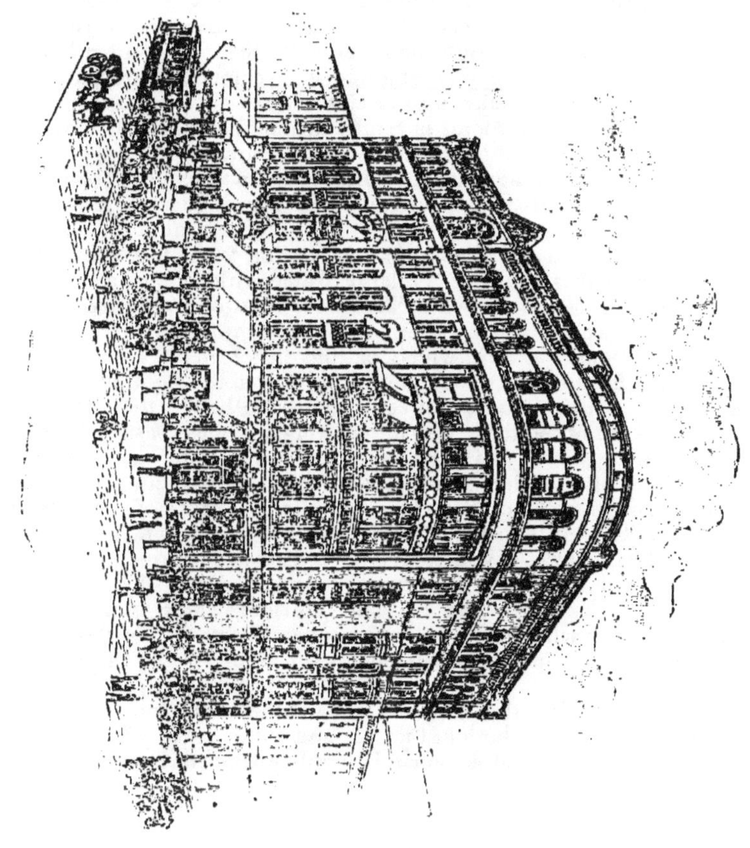

Opposite are the offices of A. E. McCann, rooms 8 and 9. One more point on the second floor is that of Frank Heslan who occupies a boot-blacking stand where the occupants of the building can avail themselves at all times of the day of his services. Directly to the left of the staircase on the second floor is S. B. Harris, one of Lowell's energetic real estate men who occupies office No. 4. In the same office is located N. W. Norcross & Co., who represent the Home Insurance Company of New York, and who do a thriving business in the underwriting line. C. E. Townsend is also an occupant of room 4 and represents the Equitable Life Insurance Company, of Lowell, and is a hustler from the word go in the insurance line.

That completes the second floor. Ascending to the third floor, the first sign that meets your eye is that of Charles W. Eaton, banker and broker, also notary public, who occupies room 30. Directly opposite is located the office of the Mutual Life Insurance Company of New York of which C. B. Wetherby is agent, occnpying room 42. As you turn to your right and walk down the right-hand corridor the well-known School of Shorthand and Stenography of which Miss Decombe is principal, will be found which helps to make up the educational advantages of Lowell. Opposite is situated the rooms of Sanborn, the photographer, who makes a specialty of all fine photographic work, occupying offices 35, 36 and 37, after which you follow up the corridor again where can be seen the sign of the Erie Telephone Company, who occupy rooms 49, 50, 51 and 52. Directly opposite is the dress-making establishment of E. M. Grogan who occupies rooms 45, 46 and 47. Ascending to the top floor, the first object which strikes your eye is a large frame which holds a large number of fine photos, some of which are of the most distinguished people in the city of Lowell, taken by Wescott. Directly off to the right is situated his handsome parlor in which patrons sit for pictures, in the rear of which is the finishing or retouching room, and to the right is situated his mailing and delivery room; directly across the hall is the art room in which are some of the most elegant paintings, frames, pastels, water colors, and to the left of the same, is located a fine show case which contains samples of his work, and directly in the rear is located a fine office. As you again go to the center of the hall the next office of importance is that of the Lowell Board of Trade; adjoining the same is the Lowell Stenography Institute, of which Miss M.A. Goodale is principal, and conducts the school under the most modern principles and success is assured her. Directly down to the left-hand corridor can be seen the sign of Merrill & Cutler who are Lowell's famous architects. The design across the entrance of their offices is well worth seeing, being bridged with fine lattice work and carving of the most beautiful style. This well-known house of Merrill & Cutler has made the plans and drawings for many public buildings, both in this city and out of town. They are both live business men and the house is highly esteemed by all who know them.

ALBERT S. FOX,

Confectionery and Candy, 58 Central St.

This well known confectionery house has been in existence about four years and has enjoyed a fast growing business ever since. Mr. Fox gives the business his personal attention and with three assistants he manufactures the products, and his sales have become famous through the manufacture of certain brands of candy. He has a finely appointed store at 58 Central street, where young ladies are in attendance during the day, and evening on Monday, Friday and Saturday. The interior is attractively arranged with all conveniences for catering, and he makes a specialty of manufacturing ice cream at wholesale, most efficient delivery being guaranteed. His past experience in catering among the leading societies, associations and private familes of the city and his fair, square dealings have gained for him the reputation like no other in the city of Lowell, for the quality of his ice cream is superior to any manufactured in Lowell. Relations with this house will prove the truth of the above statement. Mr. Fox is an energetic business man always ready to support the industrial and commercial interests of Lowell.

GEORGE LORANGER,

Merchant Tailor, Associate Building.

Within recent years, great progress has been made in hand made tailoring, and one who can speak from experience is the well known merchant tailor, George Loranger, who now occupies a handsome site in the Associate Building. He has had an experience in this line for about 29

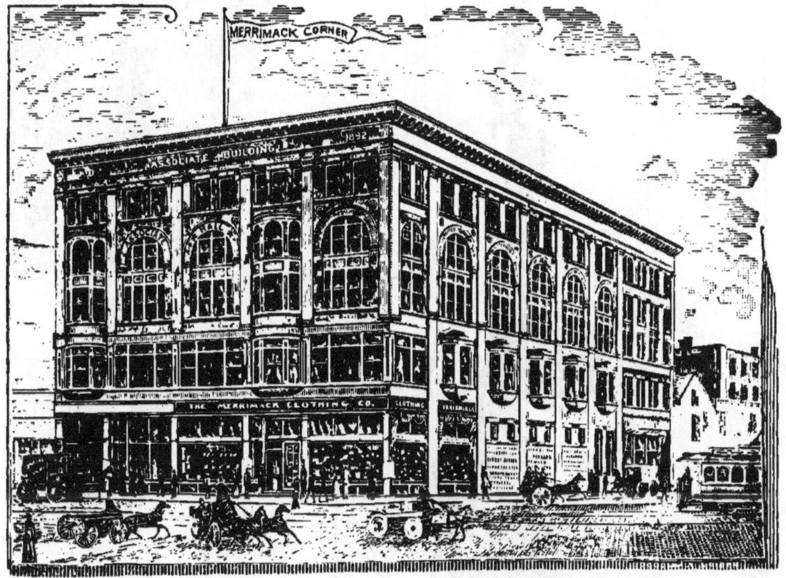

years. He is a native of Quebec, Canada, and about forty years of age. He has surely made a reputation for himself in his wide experience and can thoroughly be relied upon in his judgement of style, as he is in close connection with originators and is posted "up to-date." There cannot

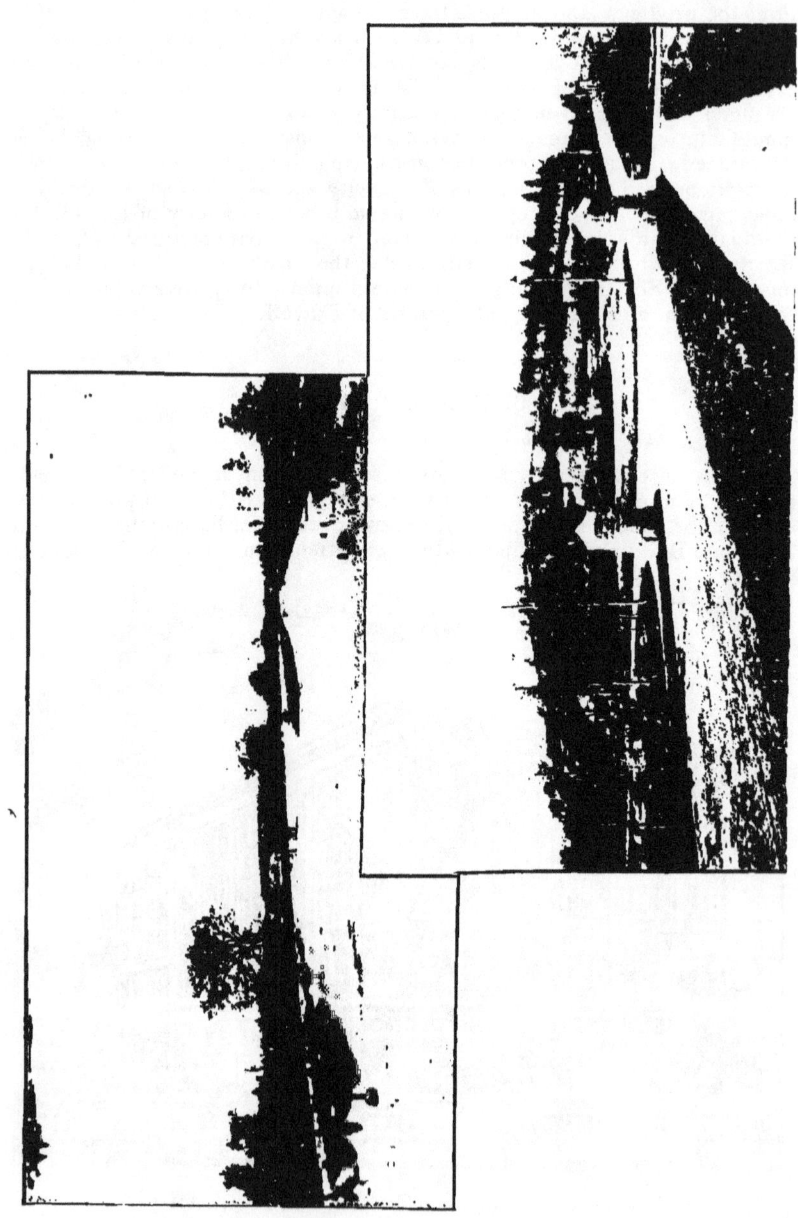

Lowell Boulevard. Fort Hill.

be too much said about his rooms, as a business site, for it is in one of the finest appointed buildings, directly opposite Monument Square, which has an elevator connection; his place is directly at the head of the staircase. Mr. Loranger is his own cutter, therefore, the most difficult part of the business is the labor of his own hands. which is a guarantee of good work as a result of his long experience and practical knowledge of the business. His line embraces every description of patterns and styles, and repairing is promptly and neatly executed at moderate rates. His place of business is open Monday, Wednesday, Friday and Saturday evenings, at which time he will be pleased to show samples to the fall trade whether they are ready to purchase or not.

This young tailoring house is sure of success with such a pushing, business man behind it as Mr. Loranger, for his judgement, vigor and experience places him in a position to give his customers the very best advantages that can possibly be offered anywhere.

J. C. BENNETT,

Hardware, Paints, and Oils, 269 Dutton St.

Among the enterprising business firms of Lowell which deserve a place in the front ranks of the large mercantile houses, is the well established house of J. C. Bennett, who began business in this city in 1866 at 200 Dutton street, in a small store, the building being a wooden story and a half structure, and his line of goods at that time consisting of a patent washing machine, clothes wringers and dryers, and he also did outside jobs of small carpenter work. In the year of 1870 Mr. Bennett moved up Dutton street to 269. into another small store, also a wooden structure, the size of which was 18 x 18 feet; from that time his business grew so rapidly that he decided that he could do business no longer in such small quarters and the small building was enlarged, giving more sales and storage rooms. He continued his business for several years with these facilities and again outgrew his quarters, and this time he erected the fine, two story brick building which now stands at the above number, 269 Dutton street, the size of which is 23 x 27, with two floors and basement of the same dimensions. His line of goods today embraces a general and complete line of builder's hardware, carpenters', machinists' and blacksmiths' tools, horseshoes and horseshoe nails, carriage bolts, light malleable carriage iron, full line of wooded basket ware, table and pocket cutlery, butchers' tools, scales and weights, and in fact anything one could expect to find in a hardware store, will be found in this well known house. He makes a specialty of the American Clothes' Dryer, which takes the lead of all others on the market; he still continues to do small jobs of carpenter work and repairing clothes dryers, wringers and carpet sweepers, and all domestic articles needing his services. Satisfaction and honest dealing have been the principles by which this house has attained its success, and business relations with it will not only prove to your advantage in honorable dealing, but also in prices.

Fiske Building.

LOWELL DENTAL ROOMS,

Located in the Fiske Building, 219 Central street, are the most pleasant and most conveniently arranged Dental Rooms outside of Boston. The name of Lowell Dental Rooms was adopted by Dr. Edwin H. Simmons in 1882, and it has become a househould name, as the Dr. has been a constant newspaper advertiser, fully believing that whatever you have to offer the public whether it be shoes or teeth, advertising is the only way to reach the public.

The Dental Art has made wondrous progress in the past few years, and the dentist to be successful is obliged to keep posted in all the new appliances that are adopted by the profession. Improvements have been made in every branch of the dental science, especially so in the making of artificial teeth, which has become a distinct branch of manufacture. There are five large manufactories in the United States which make thousands of sets of teeth annually. This work was formerly done by the dentist. The material used in the manufacture of artificial teeth are: Kaolin, Silica, Feldspar, Itanium, Oxide and preparations of platinum. Gold, iron and cobalt are used for coloring. Artificial teeth were once considered a luxury and only the well-to-do could afford them. Today there are but few families where some of them do not wear artificial teeth.

The construction of the teeth is an operation of great importance, and it requires skill and knowledge on the part of each dentist.

Dr. Simmons has given a large share of his time to this branch of dentistry, knowing that their utility depends upon proper construction and correct application. Hundreds of sets have been made by Dr. Simmons and they are being worn by his patients in Lowell and the surrounding towns, and an invitation is extended to the public to visit the Lowell Dental rooms, when in need of dentistry.

W. H. SPALDING & CO.

W. H. Spalding & Co., located in the Fiske Building, 223 Centra St., (a cut of which you will observe elsewhere) are the leading and well-known dealers in wall paper and decorating, and they also make a specialty of window screens and are a highly esteemed house in the city of Lowell.

J. CLARK GLIDDEN,

Globe Shoe Store, 225 Central St.

The desire of this leading house is to impress upon the minds of the public that prices and goods are always in harmony with quality at this store. The business is managed by the proprietor who is thoroughly conversant with the influences of the trade, and who does a business upon honor and merit, rather than misrepresentations.

PUBLIC MARKET AND PACKING COMPANY.

One of the largest emporiums in the New England states in the line of meats, groceries, provisions etc., is the well-known Public Market and

Packing Company, which is located at Nos. 72, 74, 76, and 78 Prescott street, near junction of Central. We will give you a slight description of this place in general. First, is its location which is most central and commanding: the interior of this double establishment, is about 150 feet square and employment is given to 20 skilled butchers and grocers; ten delivery wagons afford the most efficient delivery. The store keeps a fine line of cheese, butter, eggs and is furnished with lard chests and a refrigerator whose capacity is enormous. It is also equipped with the Lamson Cash Carrier system, and is lighted with electricity. It has about 90 feet front all of which is large plate glass. Lately they have added to their already immense store a grocery and provision department, which is conducted on the latest and most modern principles, having Mr. O. Brando for manager. Mr. Samuel P. Pike, is president, Mr. Burnett B. Haite, treasurer and Jerome A. Robbins, secretary.

This famous house was incorporated June, 10, 1890, with a capital of $250,000. The packing house is at St. Joseph, Montana. Beef, poultry and receivers of butter, eggs and cheese, is their line. They have branches in the following places; store No. 1, 880 to 894 Washington St., Boston, Oscar Swanson, manager; store No. 2, 1210 Tremont St. Boston, Mass., E. B. Pike, manager; store No. 3, 71, to 78 Prescott St., Lowell, Mass., F. O. Brando, manager; store No. 4 Middlesex St., Cor. Howard St., Lowell, Robert A. Moore, manager; store No. 6, 1018, and 1022 Elm St., Manchester, N. H., Fred W. Barlow, manager: store No. 7, 499 Essex St., Lawrence, Mass., A. H. McKenzie, manager; store No. 8, 1031 Elm St. Lawrence, Mass., R. J. McKenzie, manager. These are a few of the eastern branches of this famous butcher and packing enterprise and the energy and enterprise exhibited in the conduct of this house from its inception have resulted in a marked growth and substantial success, and the high esteem in which it is held by the trade for fair and honorable dealings, places it in the front ranks of Lowell's living houses.

MANSUR BROTHERS.

65 Concord Street.

One of the most recent establishments in Ward 9 is that of Mansur Brothers, who conduct and carry on a live butcher business at 65 Concord St. Established a year and a half ago, their business has constantly increased until at present they have an immense business which requires the assistance of three men. They have an efficient delivery system and sell only reliable meats, vegetables, etc., at reasonable prices. Mansur Brothers are well known throughout the city through which their large trade extends, and their fast growing business has only been the result of progressive management, with ample facilities for enlargement.

Their location is very roomy, the place being equipped with modern ice chests, knives, saws, benches, meat tables, fish tables, office, etc. They serve their products to some of the noted and first families of the city of Lowell, and have made for themselves a reputation alike noted for their first class business conducted by "up-to-date" business men.

NEW YORK CLOAK & SUIT CO,.

12 John St.

A specialty—Cloak, Suit and Furnishing house—enjoying one of the largest trade connections of any house in New England, and few if any similar stores in the country have developed greater capacity for this business.

Six year's ago Mr. J. A. Story, then of New York, selected Lowell as the centre of a highly prosperous and extensive manufacturing community, and offering the most advantageous field for an enterprise of this kind. Consequently, selecting a store in the most central business portion of the city, No. 12 John St., filling it with the newest and most approved styles of ladies' tailor-made suits, ladies' and children's garments being bought direct from the originators of styles in New York and Philadelphia, the business has proved a brilliant success from the first day he opened his doors. The situation of the store is most central and commands the eye of the public at all times. As this firm has direct communication of six years standing with the best manufacturing houses of New York, they can offer their customers advantages which cannot be obtained either in this city or in Boston.

As a convenience to their trade they have established telephone connection which number is 373-5, and such careful judgement do they use at all times in selecting their stock that the public are just as sure to be pleased by telephoning them for an article, as they would be in calling and selecting it. This substantial house will doubtless long continue to retain the high position it now occupies, which may justly be said to be the past record of an energetic, liberal and progressive business policy.

U. S. CARTRIDGE COMPANY.

C. A. R. Dimon, Agent; Paul Butler, Treas.

Make all kinds of Metallic, Pistol and Rifle cartridges, and paper shot shells.

Wallace & Sons, 29 Chambers St., New York. Chas. Sonntag & Co., San Francisco, Cal.

Pillings Shoe Factory Birds' Eye View of Collinsville Factories.

THOMAS M. BOLTON,

Saddlery and Harness Manufacturing.

An enterprise that contributes not a little to the development of the industrial resources of Lowell, and a leading one of its kind, is the establishment of Thomas M. Bolton, Saddlery, Harness, and Paraphernalia manufacturer, which was instituted about sixteen years ago at 116 Market street, where his business has steadily grown. The reputation of his products demanded a more roomy place and today he occupies two spacious places. His sale and harness department at 311 Market street as manufacturer of society paraphernalia is located on Worthen street. He now gives employment to four girls and six men at his factory.

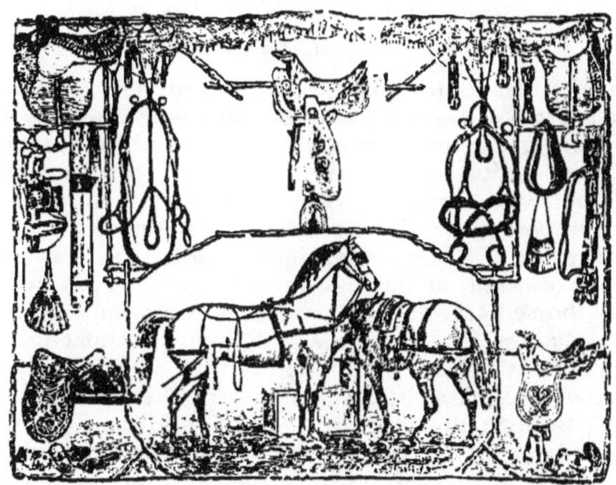

Mr. Bolton is the sole proprietor. He also handles horse furnishings, such as blankets, robes, surcingles, saddlery, etc. He carries an extensive stock of assorted fine whips and everything appertaining to the trade of foreign and domestic goods, and is the only house in Lowell which manufactures a riding saddle.

The advantages this house has to offer are good value at close prices, fine workmanship in harmony with fine quality of stock. Mr. Bolton is a practical harness maker, having learned his trade from his father when a very young man, and his experience in fine work for society paraphernalia is gaining for him an increase of trade in that direction.

C. H. KIMBALL,

119 Central St.

C. H. Kimball, a respected merchant of the city of Lowell, has long been connected with the clothing business, being located at 119 Central street. Mr. Kimball is an old resident of Lowell and has built for himself through honest and square dealings an all round trade. He is welknown among the G. A. R. men, of which he is one. He has done business in a small store with small windows for the past ten years, and if a person were to pass his place of business today they will find it much changed. The goods are always in keeping with a house which is conducted upon thorough business principles. Mr. Kimball is widely known in public circles as having the most prominent location for a store, and as one of Lowell's prosperous merchants, which is attributed to the fact that he always gives value for money received. His attendants are all of the most agreeable type, responsible in the discharge of their duties and with the personal attention of Mr. Kimball satisfaction is always guaranteed.

J. E. CONANT & CO.,

Lowell, Mass.

An enterprise that contributes not a little to the development of the industrial resources of Lowell and a leading one of the kind in the city, is that of Conant & Company, which was instituted in 1861, and has since established a reputation for its superior standing and a trade that extends generally throughout the northern part of Massachusetts. This company, is composed of J. A. Conant, Edmund B. Conant and Henry L. Huntress. They are extensive horse and harness handlers, also jobbers of all kinds of harness furnishings, blankets, robes, surcingles, saddlery, horse hareware, etc., and they carry an extensive stock of everything pertaining to foreign and domestic manufacturers. Among some of the domestic goods they carry are from such well-known houses as Peter Calhoune & Co., Factory, Newark, New Jersey, Branch 56 Sudbury St., Boston; they are also agents for Albert J. Downing's celebrated Concord wagons, agents for the famous London harness, branch office of which is at 206 Devonshire St, Boston, which includes all parts of harness, gate saddlery, winkers, bridles, housing, blinders, halters, lines, etc., all of which are offered to the trade at prices as low as is consistent with quality. This well-known house of Conant & Company also does an auctioneer business and have become widely known through their auction sales, which include not only the sale of harness etc., but real estate. The advantages this house has to offer are many and valuable and that they are appreciated is evidence of the growth and prosperity of the enterprise. The members of the firm are all practical, experienced and progressive business men, enjoying advanced facilities and conducting their business on liberal methods. They have developed trade that is creditable to itself and the interests of this city.

CHARLES E. ADAMS.

Hardware, Paints, Oils, Glass, Varnishes & Mill Supplies.

MASSACHUSETTS STATE BOARD OF TRADE, CHARLES E. ADAMS, PRES.

This association is composed of 32 boards and mercantile organizations, representing the entire state, and is an important factor in promoting the welfare of the commercial and industrial interests of Massachusetts.

Mr. Adams is also interested in electrical matters, being president of the Bradbury-Stone Electric Storage Co., and a director in the Northwestern Telephone Exchange Co., of Minnesota, the Cleveland Telephone Co., of Cleveland, Ohio, the Southwestern Telegraph & Telephone Co., of Arkansas and Texas, and a director in the Lowell, Lawrence & Haverhill Electric Railroad. He is also a member of the Board of Investment of the Merrimack River Savings Bank; first vice-president of the National Paint, Oil & Varnish Association and United States Alternate Commissioner to the World's Columbian Exposition from Massachusetts.

LOWELL HOSIERY COMPANY.

Manufacturers of Plain and Fancy Hosiery, Mt. Vernon St.

This corporation was established and began operation in 1869. Its first officers were C. P. Talbot, brother of the late Ex-Governor Talbot, president; Ex-Mayor Hocum Hosford, treasurer; and William W. F. Salmon, manager; all of whom have since died. It is essentially a Lowell institution, almost all of its stock being owned in this city, and it has had connected with it some of Lowell's most prominent men.

This company, while making a grade of hosiery suited to the popular purse, have always maintained a high reputation for the excellence of their goods, and were awarded the medal of the Centennial Exhibition of 1876, for their high standard in this respect. For the past few years the demand has been for black hosiery and this company has been running almost entirely on their "Fast Blacks." They have had very large sales on these goods, and, although dyeing all colors, their fast black continues to be the bulk of their production. They take raw cotton as it comes from the South, and turn it into any color or style of stocking desired. Connected with the mills is a bleachery, where besides their own work, they do the bleaching of several of the other knit goods mills of this city. The present officials are: Arthur G. Pollard, president; James Duckworth, treasurer, and W. A. Eastman, superintendent. The goods are all sold through the well known house of Bliss, Fabyan & Co., Boston, New York, Philadelphia and Baltimcre.

A. H. CLUER,

Dealer in Light and Heavy Express Driving Harness.

The most famous harness establishment in the city of Lowell is without a doubt the well known establishment of A. H. Cluer, located at No. 340 Bridge street, Centralville. He was formerly established in 1887 at 70 Bridge street; served his apprenticeship in Littleton, Mass., and is a native of Stoughton, Mass. This live house employs five skilled workmen and manufactures all grades of light and heavy harness, which can be had from $9.00 to $100. The question has been asked what has made this house so famous. The answer is, its prices, for it has the reputation of selling more harnesses than any other two houses in Lowell, at prices in keeping with first class workmanship, quality, make, style, etc., which are sure to please and are of superior quality. His line also embraces blankets, whips, combs, brushes, etc. Think of a breast plate harness, single or double strapped, machine sewed, 5-8 inches, either style check with 3½ inch saddle, reins, russett or black, trusses 1-1 1-8 inches, single or double strap, trimmed with nickel-ware or imitation rubber, seam pattern, for $9.00. He also manufactures a breast carryall harness for $12.00, guaranteed in every particular. A carryall hame harness for $15.00 coupe hame harness, hame double strap and machine sewed, coupe style, $20.00, and a fine light grocery express harness for $17.00.

No single house in the city of Lowell can understand how his reputation has been made. Look on the inside of the first page and see why.

Mr. Cluer is steady at work keeping the people thinking how he can sell harnesses warranted, guaranteed and satisfactory in every respect, at small prices, but as the time goes on and you become acquainted with this famous house and have business relations with it you will learn its value, its honorable dealings, its business principles, its workmanship, and its prices cannot fail to impress one favorably.

Mr. Cluer is an "up-to-date" experienced harness manufacturer in every sense of the word, having learned the trade and, he has, and will keep, the people thinking of his line of goods at prices which are a wonder. He is a progressive merchant closely identified with the industrial and commercial interest and advancement of Lowell.

HARRY RAYNES,

Jeweler, 69 Central St.

This enterprise was originally established by Joseph Raynes, July, 1831, who was a native of York, Maine, and conducted the business in what was known at that time as a ten footer, the building being very small and low. In 1860. G. W. Raynes was added to the concern which changed its name to Joseph Raynes & Co. Joseph Raynes died Feb. 17, 1879, and again the concern was changed and called Raynes Brothers. In Dec. 1881, the firm was again dissolved and Harry Raynes took full possession of the business which has, since that time, under his personal observation, been very successful. Harry Raynes is a native of Lowell and possesses a wide experience in the jewelry business of something over 30 years.

This well known and esteemed house has maintained a steady growth of business since its birth, and is known not only as a local concern but throughout all the surrounding towns. The main salesroom at 69 Central street contains a complete assortment of jewelry, silver ware and everything appertaining to the jewelry line. The stock is complete at all times. Mr. Raynes is not a figure head of the concern but is a practical jeweler, his long experience giving him great knowledge of buying goods, which places his line in the front ranks, and enables him to give the public the most advantageous bargains. Mr. Raynes is an enterprising business man, and is closely identified with Lowell's commercial and industrial growth. He is highly esteemed and a believer in a liberal, business policy.

F. H. PEARSON & CO.,

120 & 122 Merrimack St.

The name of the 20th Century Shoe Store has become one of the most famous of all names or titles of commercial establishments. This house of which F. H. Pearson & Co. are proprietors, has gained a wide reputation as the largest human shoers outside of the metropolis. Their motto, "a fit or no sale," has, without a doubt, with their fair dealing methods, done greatly toward building up this immense business. But when we stop to think that the business is personally conducted and managed by Mr. Pearson in the selection of the stock, who is capable in every respect of knowing the wants of the people in general, their success is not sur-

prising. They carry such a stock that will catch the eye of the public both in price and quality. They have certainly done a great deal to bring about competition, and no house in Lowell shows any finer stock with harmonized prices; no greater varieties have been shown in the larger cities, and this simple fact with the steady growth of this house can be laid at the door of its management, who have only the latest and most modern business principles and original ideas of window trimming; with polite, genial clerks, with well assorted, reserved stock, and with their motto of a "fit or no sale" they cannot fail to please. Their location is most central, being very attractively appointed inside and out, and without a doubt is the most popular shoe house in the city of Lowell. Their line embraces everything in footwear and the advantages in inducements offered to the public by this house are also available to surrounding environs. Concerning the reliability and honor of this firm, comment would be impertinent, its high standing, prominent success and magnitude of operation being ample evidence of the character of its business policy.

Mr. F. H. Pearson, the proprietor, began his shoe experience in the year of 1881 in the month of April, in a shoe factory at Haverhill, Mass. The following year, in 1882, Feb. 20, he was burnt out by a large fire in Haverhill, and in 1883 was employed by Mr. E. H. Adams; served him until the business took a change to Mitchell & Co., and continued the same with Mitchell & Co., until June 1892, at which time birth was given to the 20th Century Shoe Store, and which has since been conducted by him.

M. A. FOGG & CO.

Parlor & Chamber Furniture, 458 Central Street.

This firm, located at 458 Central St., has been doing business for nearly six years, and through honest and square dealings in all its transactions, and strict attention to business has built up a trade that is fast increasing, and coming into the front rank among the many business houses in Lowell.

They handle a first-class line of house furniture, carpets, oil cloth, bedding, crockery and tinware, and are also sellers of the Fogg's "Beauty" & Fogg's "Jewel" Ranges, which are made expressly for them by the famous Somerset Stove Foundry Co., which is one of the oldest foundries in New England.

If you are in need of anything in the housekeeping line, you will do well to call and inspect their stock of goods, for they maintain their reputation for low prices, and first-class goods and they are sure to please you.

LOWELL CEMETERY.

1895.

President, Henry H. Wilder, treasurer, Charles L. Knapp, Middlesex Safe Deposit & Trust Co.. Cor. Merrimack & Palmer Sts. Board of Trustees, Francis Jewett, Ethan A. Smith, August Fels, Charles A. Stott, William H. Wiggin, Larkin T. Trull, Charles L. Hildreth, Zina E. Stone, Leavitt R. J. Varnum, Albert Pinder, D. Moody Prescott, James L. Campbell. Superintendent, Robert Mulno.

MIDDLESEX SAFE DEPOSIT AND TRUST CO.

Merrimack St., Cor. Palmer.

This company is authorized by law to receive and execute trusts of any character from courts, corporations and individuals who act as administrators, guardians, receivers, assignees, trustees, registrars and general agents, in any matter of business, and take entire charge of estates, real and personal. It is subject to examination by the state bank commissioner.

President, Larkin T. Trull; directors, Miles F. Brennan, J. A. Coram, W. H. I. Hayes, August Fels. Patrick Kelley, Charles F. Kelley, Thomas F. Morris, Charles D. Palmer, Percy Parker, Peter H. Donahue, Stephen B. Puffer, John P. Pilling, George E. Putnam, J. A. Shanley, E. A. Smith, E. W. Thomas, Larkin T. Trull, E. M. Tucke, Fred T. Walsh; treasurer, Charles L. Knapp. Bank of Deposit and Safety Deposit boxes to rent.

HALL & MAYOTTE,

Tailors, Hildreth Building.

The liveliest enterprise in the merchant tailoring line is the house of Hall & Mayotte, which was established in 1884, and has since developed a flattering patronage among the best dressed and most distinguished citizens of Lowell and vicinity. The salesroom occupied is one of the most attractive in Lowell. It is handsomely appointed, is lighted by three large plate glass windows on the second floor, and in all its furnishings presents an air of refinement and good taste fully in accord with the superior quality of fabrics exhibited. The goods embrace a valuable assortment of Parisian and domestic woolens, tweeds, worsteds and novelties in fashionable weaves, which cannot fail to please the most fastidious and most critical buyers. Mr. Mayotte is not a mere figurehead, but is a practical cutter and expert tailor of over 20 years experience, and personally attends to all the details of production, allowing no garment to leave his hands unless it can be pronounced absolutely perfect in fit, finish, workmanship, style, trimming and material. The house has a liberal patronage and is surely a popular one, and it may be emphatically relied upon to furnish only such garments as shall be first class in every respect.

Mr. Mayotte well deserves the success he has attained, and he may be properly ranked as one of the leading tailors of the New England states, as well as a progressive, energetic business man.

A. H. SANBORN.

Photographer, 53 Central St. Central Block

This photographic enterprise was established in 1885, and in the onward progress of Lowell's commercial supremacy, has long fulfilled in an acceptable manner its mission in providing the trade and customers with the most reliable goods of the kind in the market, making a specialty of photographic goods, and doing a fine art work in the reproduction of machinery, furniture and everything in that important line.

Mr. Sanborn established in business over a quarter of a century ago, and during all these years has enjoyed a large and annually increasing trade, which extends throughout the city and surrounding towns, having been the result of the adoption of new and advanced methods and enterprise on the part of Mr. Sanborn.

The premises occupied for the business are centrally located and handsomely appointed, being a part of the immense Central Block in which so many enterprises are located.

He is a native of Auburn, New Hampshire, and has been closely identified with the progress of Lowell for many years. In all respects this house occupies a commanding position in the trade and offers advantages and benefits to buyers difficult to procure elsewhere in the city.

F. W. SHERMAN,

Insurance.

This Insurance Agency is a valuable and great benefactor to the commercial interests of the city of Lowell, and its reputation is maintained by avoiding any methods that promise economy at the cost of quality, representing as they do only thoroughly reliable companies. Therefore it naturally enjoys the patronage of the leading commercial and manufacturing concerns of this community. Mr. Sherman is an enterprising business man and is closely identified with the growth and advancement of Lowell. He is highly esteemed in the community for liberal business dealings and he justly invites the influential patronage secured by his energy and enterprise.

AMERICAN FIRE INSURANCE COMPANY.

This insurance agency is remarkable for its monstrous growth and illustrates what can be brought about by close application to business and reliable dealings with customers. Mr. Sherman commenced business with the agency of only one company, the "Ins," in 1883, and continued to add companies to his agency, until 1892 their joint agency, with the old Geo. W. Coburn Insurance Agency, which represented the "Old Worcester" Mutual, assumed large proportions. His next move was to buy out the agency, which Mr. Sherman did on Jan. 17, 1895, and he now controls and represents the following list of stock and Mutual Companies:

Franklin of Philadelphia, American Fire of Philadelphia, Glen Falls of N. Y., Norwich Union of London, Eng., Sun Insurance Office of London, Eng., Firemen's of New Jersey, American of New Jersey, Orient of Hartford, Conn., United States of N. Y., American of N. Y., American of Boston, Security of New Haven, Conn., Union of Philadelphia, Spring Garden of Philadelphia, Metropolitan Plate Glass of N. Y., London Guarantee & Accident Co. Eng., Standard Life & Accident Co., Detroit, Worcester Mutual, Traders & Mechanics Mutual and Dorchester Mutual.

W. A. DICKINSON.

Manufauturer of Soap, Cor. Howard & Tanner Sts.

An old and well-established house is that of W. A. Dickinson who is a manufacturer of scouring, filling, laundry and toilet soaps, also a dealer in tallows etc. The works are located at the corner of Howard and Tanner Sts., where is carried on a business of prime tallow, caustic soda, sal soda, soda-ash and resin for the purpose of reproducing soaps of all kinds. This well-known house is one of long standing and is located at the central part of the manufacturing district, and has enjoyed a continuous growth for the past ten years. Its proprietor, Mr. Dickinson, is a man of wide scope of business experience and is closely identified with the commercial and industrial interests in this and other cities. He is a man of liberal thought in public matters and is possessed of a commodious factory wherein the goods are manufactured. The building is about 150 x 80 feet, two stories high, with basement.

His trade extends not only locally, but throughout New England. The railroad facilities are unsurpassed, having close connection within ten feet of the rear of the factory, where goods are shipped and unloaded. Mr. Dickinson gives employment to many hands who are skilled in the manufacture of soap and handling ot raw product. This establishment has grown to be a public benefactor in relation to the city's interest, and is ranked in the front tier of factories of its kind, and Lowell is proud to show that some of the finest powdered, scouring, filling, laundry soaps are the product and manufacture of Lowell's industry.

DANIEL GAGE,

Coal, Wood and Ice.

One of the largest and most successful merchants in the coal, wood and ice business in the city of Lowell, is Daniel Gage, who has the largest ice depositories in the state outside of those controlled by the Boston Ice Co. He has fourteen buildings two stories high, 50 x 14 feet. His barns, alone cover an acre of land, in which is kept no less than 100 horses, his trade extending throughout the environs of Lowell, giving employment to about 80 hands who are all experienced in their various departments. He is a large real estate owner and is closely identified with the commercial and industrial interests, all of which are concentrated in Lowell. The public in general have always placed great confidence in this well-known establishment, which has obtained the same only by adopting honorable methods in selling, by reasonable prices and acting in an accommodating manner, for all of which this house is noted.

Mr. Gage is a broad, public spirited man and a live merchant in every sense of the word. No such business could have been attained without the most progressive kind of management such as has resulted in business with Daniel Gage.

JAMES McKINLEY,

Fancy and Staple Groceries.

Pawtucketville merchants are coming to the front among the live business men of Lowell, the well known house of James McKinley, being without doubt the largest in that section. He was established in 1886 in a small way, and has enjoyed a steady growth of business ever since; he is a native of Lowell and has been a candidate for overseer of the poor. His line embraces a complete stock of first class groceries, such as teas, coffees, spices; he also conducts a feed, hay and grain business at the same place, 42 to 48 Mammoth Road, corner Clifton Ave.

He gives employment to four clerks in the store and others outside; he has an efficient delivery system of three teams; he is a man who has many friends in Lowell and vicinity, and is known to be a thorough business man of conservative principles, and with honorable dealing has gained the immense business reputation this house has; every article which leaves his store is first class and prices are always in harmony with such goods. All are invited to try the same and be convinced of the truth of the above statements.

BARTLETT & DOW,

Hardware, 128, 132 and 134 Central St.

Among the leading retail and wholesale hardware dealers of the country, none have attained a higher position in their line of business than Bartlett & Dow, who are sole agents in Lowell for many articles of hardware, mechanics' tools, cutlery, milk pails, milking stools, agricultural implements, firemen's requisites, mill and machine shop supplies, asbestos goods, French and German toys, etc. No house in the city has a wider reputation than this, which has attained the highest standard of perfection both in methods of management, resources and supply, foundation of experience and practical knowledge in the business.

This house has in reserved stock at all times every conceivable article which a person would only look to a hardware dealer for. The proprietors, Messrs. Bartlett & Dow, are well known throughout the state, and it has been said that no house in the metropolis is better known as a local concern than this establishment. Their premises are large and spacious, occupying a five story brick structure with 60 feet frontage, and is equipped with all modern improvements, such as elevator, electric lights, handsome offices, cash carrier system, perfectly kept stock, and fine storage room, each department separately managed by experienced individuals, in all employing twenty hands, having efficient delivery teams in which goods are promptly delivered. This house is headquarters for contractors' and builders' supplies, and their prices are in keeping with first class goods at contractors' rates. Farmers seek Bartlett and Dow for farming implements, rakes, hoes, shovels, etc.; in fact the name "Bartlett & Dow" has become so widely known that every child knows its location. Honorable methods only being employed, it has made them famous and successful.

DR. CHADBOURNE.

Francis Watts Chadbourne, son of Francis Watts and Eliza (Bacon) Chadbourne, was born in Kennebunk, Maine. He entered Bowdoin College in 1863, and at the end of the sophomore year, entered the United States service as hospital steward, which position he filled to the end of the war of the Rebellion. He studied medicine at the Portland School for Medical Instruction, attended lectures at Bowdoin, receiving his degree from the latter institution in May, 1869, after which he pursued special courses in chemistry and botany at Bowdoin, and then attended a year's course at Harvard.

Dr. Chadbourne commenced practice in Orono and Oldtown, Maine, remaining there until 1876 when he moved to Lowell. While in Maine he was superintendent of schools, which office he held until his removal to Massachusetts. He was also Assistant Surgeon to the Massachusetts Volunteer Militia. He is chairman of the staff of the Corporation Hospital, also a member of the medical staff of the Lowell General Hospital. He is a member of the Massachusetts Medical Society, Commissioner (at present) of Trades for the Middlesex North District Society, also a member of the Lowell Medical Journal Club. He married June 24th, 1874, Ella Maria Whiting of Brookline, Mass.

Talbot Mills, Billerica.

Collins Mills, Collinsville.

TALBOT MILLS.

No. Billerica.

Established 1857. Incorporated 1884.

Solomon Lincoln, President. Frederick S. Clark, treasurer. Dress Goods, Cheviots, Carriage Linings, Flannels, etc.

Woolen manufacturers. Twenty Sets Cards, 10,240 Spindles, 178 Broad Looms.

Selling Agents: Parker, Wilder & Co., Boston & New York.

M. COLLINS MILLS,

Collinsville.

Among the many large concerns in New England engaged in the manufacture of textile fabrics, the M. Collins Mills, whose extensive plant is located at Collinsville, in the town of Dracut, Mass., stands pre-eminent, both in regard to the aggregate and quality of its output. This enterprise was inaugurated January 1, 1877, succeeding the Merrimack Woollen Mills, November 25, 1876, by the present proprietor, one of the most successful and enterprising among the list of successful manufacturers of this section. The business was carried on in the "Old Mill" until 1885, when the substantial new mill, which was begun in 1884, was completed. The growth of the industry necessitated extensive alterations, and in 1892 the enlargement of the "New Mill" was begun, by the addition of three stories to the entire structure, making the main building, which is two hundred and thirteen feet by sixty feet in area, six stories high, with a weave shed covering a space of one hundred and sixty-five feet attached. The plant as it now stands is one of the most complete in the country. The machinery is of the best and latest designs known to the art, and in their appointments the Collins Mills are all that mechanical engineering can suggest. The machinery is operated by both water and steam power, and a force of three hundred and fifty hands is employed in the works. The product of the Collins Mills comprises Meltons, Ladies' Cloths and Cheviots, and the specialties of the Company are Beavers and Beaver Cloakings of superior quality and finish. In all the markets of the country, the output of this great concern successfully competes with all makes of this line of goods, and the immense trade built up by Mr. M. Collins, the proprietor, is a just tribute to his business worth, energy and judgment.

L. J. AND J. A. ROGERS,

Millinery, 54 Central St. and 51 Prescott St.

No. 54 Central street is the location of one of the most central buildings, in which is located the millinery establishment of L. J. and J. A. Rogers, who were established March 14, 1895.

A few points in relation to the interior, which the passer by cannot help noticing, is the fact that it is surrounded with mirrors, having the most elegant style of decoration, and their two large show windows are always neatly dressed and very attractive. Both the Misses Rogers are practical milliners of wide experience, and are constantly in touch with original designers, who keep them posted from time to time upon the styles.

They give employment to several skilled hands in the busy season who renovate, trim and make to order, etc. The establishment is directly at the head on Middle street and opposite the Central Block, a picture of which will be found elsewhere.

This millinery house is an assured success through the instrumentality of the class of trade they attract—the best people of Lowell—who seek to buy responsible goods of responsible parties at reasonable prices. All are invited to inspect the display of millinery goods on exhibition. Kindly remember the place, Rogers' Millinery Store, 54 Central street and 51 Prescott street, where one and all are treated the same, under the progressive management of the Misses Rogers, who are assured of success in their new enterprise.

LOWELL BLEACHERY.

Incorporated Jan. 18, 1833.

Capital, - - - - - - - - $400,000.

Officers, with date of appointment.

Treasurers.		Agents.	
John Clark, - - - - - -	1833.	Jonathan Derby, - - . . -	1833.
James C. Dunn, - - - -	1834.	Joseph Hoyt, - - - - - -	1834.
Charles T. Appleton, - -	1835.	Charles T. Appleton, - -	1835.
Samuel G. Snell, - - - -	1859.	Charles A. Babcock, - -	1849.
Percival Lowell, - - - -	1886.	Fordyce Coburn, - - - -	1880.
Eliot C. Clarke. - - - - -	1889.	F. P. Appleton, - - - - -	1882.
		James N. Bourne, - - - -	1886.

Directors, 1893.

Augustus Lowell, Harrison Gardner, Geo. F. Richardson, Francis C. Gray, Eliot C. Clarke.

Annual Meeting, Third Monday in July.

LAWRENCE MANUFACTURING CO.

Incorporated 1831.

Present Capital, - - - - - - $1,500,000.

Treasurers.		Agents.	
William Appleton, - - - -	1831.	William Austin, - - - -	1830.
Henry Hall, - - - - - - -	1832.	John Aiken, - - - - - - -	1837.
Henry V. Ward, - - - -	1857.	William S, Southworth, -	1849.
T. Jefferson Coolidge, -	1868.	William F. Salmon, - - - -	1865.
Lucius M. Sargent, - -	1880.	Daniel Hussey, - - - - -	1869.
		John Kilburn, - - - - -	1878.

Cotton cloth of various grades was for a long series of years the only article of manufacture. In 1864 the manufacture of cotton hosiery for women was begun and that class of goods has since been an important product of the company.

JEREMIAH CLARK,

Cotton and Woolen Machinery.

Every old resident of Lowell has known or heard of Jere. Clark, who is an extensive dealer in all kinds of cotton and woolen machinery and supplies. His office is located at 77 Dutton St., opposite Lowell Machine Shop, but it necessitates a visit to his five storehouses, covering over two acres of floor surface to gain any adequate idea of the vastness of his enterprise. A machine repair shop is also run in connection with

the storehouses, which employs several hands. Mr. Clark is also president of the Mechanics Savings Bank, and is an exemplary citizen, though an unobtrusive one. His enterprise has been conducive of promoting the industry of the Spindle City, and he is justly entitled to the prestige he has gained in the city of his residence.

BOOTT COTTON MILLS.

Incorporated, 1835. Began work 1836.

Present capital, - - - - - $1,200,000.

Treasurers.		Agents.	
John Amory Lowell, - -	1835.	Benjamin F. French, - -	1836.
J. Pickering Putnam, - -	1848.	Linus Child, - - - - - -	1847.
T. Jefferson Coolidge, - -	1858.	William A. Burke, - - -	1862.
Richard J. Rogers, - - -	1865.	Alexander G. Cumnock, -	1868.
Augustus Lowell, - - -	1875.		
Eliot C. Clarke, - - - -	1886.		

Gallons oil per year, - - - - - - 12,000.
Pounds starch per year, - - - - - - 300,000.
Water wheels, 1 6 Ft. 8 in., & 8 6 Ft.
Steam power, - - - 4 engines, 2000 horse-power.

DIRECTORS, 1893.

Augustus Lowell, president; Eliot C. Clarke, treasurer; C. William Loring, Arthur T. Lyman, Edward W. Hooper, Augustus Flagg, Edward I. Browne.

Annual meeting, last week in May.

Eliot C. Clarke, treasurer, Boston; A. G. Cumnock, agent; Victor I. Cumnock, superintendent.

Capital (12000 shares; par 100) - - - -	$1,200,000.
No. Mills, - - - - - - - -	6.
Spindles, - - - - - - - -	151,292.
Looms, - - - - - - - -	4,200.
Females Employed, - - - - - -	1,500.
Males employed, - - - - - -	478.
Yards made per week, - - - - -	800,000.
Pounds cotton used per week, - - - -	215,000.

Kinds of goods made: sheetings, shirtings, printing cloth, 14 to 60.

Tons coal per year, - - - - - - 8,000.

OLD LOWELL NATIONAL BANK.

The Old Lowell National Bank, situated on Central street (between Merrimack and Middle streets), with a capital of $200,000 and surplus of $40,000, is the oldest financial institution in the city. Its charter as a state bank (called the Lowell Bank), is dated March 11, 1828, bearing the signature of Levi Lincoln, governor.

The first board of directors consisted of Nathaniel Wright, Phineas Whiting, Josiah B. French, Joshua Bennett, Benj. Varnum and J. Morse, all closely identified with the early development of the city.

One entry in the records of the bank shows how time and methods have changed. On Dec. 21, 1829, it was voted, "That all bills or money sent by the stages from this bank to the Globe Bank in Boston shall be taken from the vaults by the cashier, and delivered to the stageman the morning the stage starts."

Up to the present time the bank has had seven presidents as follows: Nathaniel Wright, who served over thirty years; Jas. G. Carney, part of one year; Dr. John O. Green, two years; Joshua Bennett, four years; Edward Tucke, over eighteen years; John Davis, eleven years; Edward Tucke (son of a former president) elected the beginning of the present year.

There have been but four cashiers, the first being James G. Carney, who filled the position over seventeen years, and whose name will always have a prominent place in the financial history of the city, David Hyde, for four years, John L. Ordway, for fourteen years, and the present cashier, Chas. M. Williams, since 1863, about thirty-two years. The board of directors (in addition to president and cashier) consists of the following: William M. Carey, manufacturer of wood working machinery; Joseph L. Chalifoux, clothing dealer; Peter H. Donahue, wholesale liquor dealer; Percy Parker, treasurer electric railway system; Geo. F. Penniman, real estate; Phineas Whiting, retired (son of member of first board) and Artemas B. Woodworth, lumber dealer.

The bank is centrally located, having moved into its present convenient and commodious quarters within a few years, and has a most honorable record for safe, conservative management.

TREMONT & SUFFOLK MILLS.

Suffolk Manufacturing Company, incorporated Jan. 17th, 1831.

Proprietors Tremont & Suffolk Mills, incorporated Mar. 19th, 1831.

Present capital, - - - - - - $1,500,000.

Officers, with date of appointment.

TREASURERS, Suffolk Manufacturing Company.

John W. Boott,	Feb. 17, 1831.
Henry Hall,	April 2, 1832.
Henry V. Ward.	April 7, 1859.
Walter Hastings,	July 10, 1865.
William A. Burke,	Feb. 4, 1868.
James C. Ayer,	Aug. 10, 1870.

TREASURERS, Proprietors of The Tremont Mills.

William Appleton,	April 9, 1831.
Henry Hall,	April 3, 1832.
Henry V. Ward,	April 7, 1859.
Walter Hastings.	July, 10, 1865.
William A. Burke,	Feb. 4, 1868.
James C. Ayer,	Aug. 10, 1870.

TREASURERS, Tremont & Suffolk Mills.

James C. Ayer,	Aug. 19, 1871.
John C. Birdseye,	March 26, 1872.
Alphonso S. Covel,	Jan. 1887.

AGENTS, Suffolk Manufacturing Company.

Robert Means,	June 13, 1871.
John Wright,	Dec. 20, 1872.
Thomas S. Shaw.	June 1, 1868.

AGENTS, Proprietors of the Tremont Mills.

Israel Whitney,	July 28, 1831.
John Aiken,	Jan. 31, 1834.
Charles L. Tilden,	June 28, 1837.
Charles F. Battles,	Oct. 16, 1858.
Thomas S. Shaw,	March 23, 1870.

AGENTS, Tremont & Suffolk Mills.

Thomas S. Shaw.	Aug. 12, 1871.
Edward W. Thomas,	June 22, 1877.

APPLETON COMPANY.

Incorporated 1828.
Present capital, - - - - - - - $600,000.
Officers, with date of appointment.

SUPERINTENDENTS.

John Avery,	1828.
George Motley,	1831.
J. H. Sawyer,	1867.
Daniel Wright,	1881.
Wm. H. McDavitt.	1887.

TREASURERS.

William Appleton,	1828.
Patrick T. Jackson,	1829.
George W. Lyman,	1832.
Thomas C. Carey,	1841.
William B. Bacon,	1859.
Arthur T. Lyman,	1861.
Arthur L. Devens,	1863.
John A. Burnham,	1867.
George Motley,	1867.
James A. Dupee, 1874,	Died Oct. 18, 1886.
Louis Robeson,	1886.

AGENT.

C. H. Richardson,	Nov. 1888.

DIRECTORS, 1893.

Edward I. Browne, S. C. Dana, Henry C. Howe, Wm. S. Appleton, J. Herbert Sawyer, Louis Robeson, Arthur G. Pollard.

Wm. S. Appleton, president; Louis Robeson, treasurer; Daniel L. Prendergast, clerk.

Annual meeting, first Wednesday in January.

Capital (600 shares; par $1000,)	$600,000.
No. mills,	6.
Spindles,	50,776.

Looms,	1,610.
Females employed,	600.
Males employed,	420.
Yards made per week,	313,000.
Pounds cotton used per week,	122,000.

Kind of goods made, sheetings shirtings, drillings, flannelettes, dress goods and tickings.

Tons coal per year,	3,650.
Gallons oil per year,	7,200.
Pounds starch per year,	140,000.
Water wheels,	5 Turbines.
Steam power,	2 engines, 100 horse-power.

MERRIMACK MANUFACTURING COMPANY.

Incorporated, 1822.

Present capital, - - - - - - $2,500,000.

Howard Stockton, treas.; John J. Hart, supt. of Print Works; John W. Pead, supt. of Mills; Joseph S. Ludlam, agent.

The mills and storehouses of this company are located on the bank of the Merrimack river, extending from the waste-way separating their property from that of the Boot Cotton Mills on the east, to Tilden St. on the west,—the Print Works extending from the river, between Prince and Tilden Sts., to the foot of Colburn St. The boarding houses are situated between Moody St. and the mills, on Dutton, Worthen and Colburn Sts.

E. P. McCOY,

Thorndike St.

An old establishment of importance in the wagon building, blacksmith and horse shoeing industry is the well known concern of E. P. McCoy. The original plant was occupied by Bird & McCoy, the partnership being dissolved later. Mr. McCoy is at present sole owner and proprietor. He has also another establishment at 36 Mammoth Road, Pawtucketville. Mr. McCoy is a native of Canada and has resided in Lowell since 1858, and has built up for himself a most prosperous business, giving the business his personal attention. He is an experienced blacksmith and knows the ins and outs of the entire business. His establishment is centrally located on Thorndike street, where is carried on the horse shoeing business, general blacksmithing, wagon building, repairing, painting, etc.

The floorage of the building covers about a half acre of land. Mr. McCoy employs about fifteen hands in the busy season, all of whom are skilled workmen. He is thoroughly equipped with the most approved machinery and adequately fitted for handling the different lines of trade which he has built up. He has recently opened a branch business at 36 Mammoth Road, where a large horse shoeing and repairing business is carried on. Mr. McCoy is well acquainted in the city and surrounding territories, and his business is constantly increasing and he solely attributes his success to the fine workmanship in all his departments.

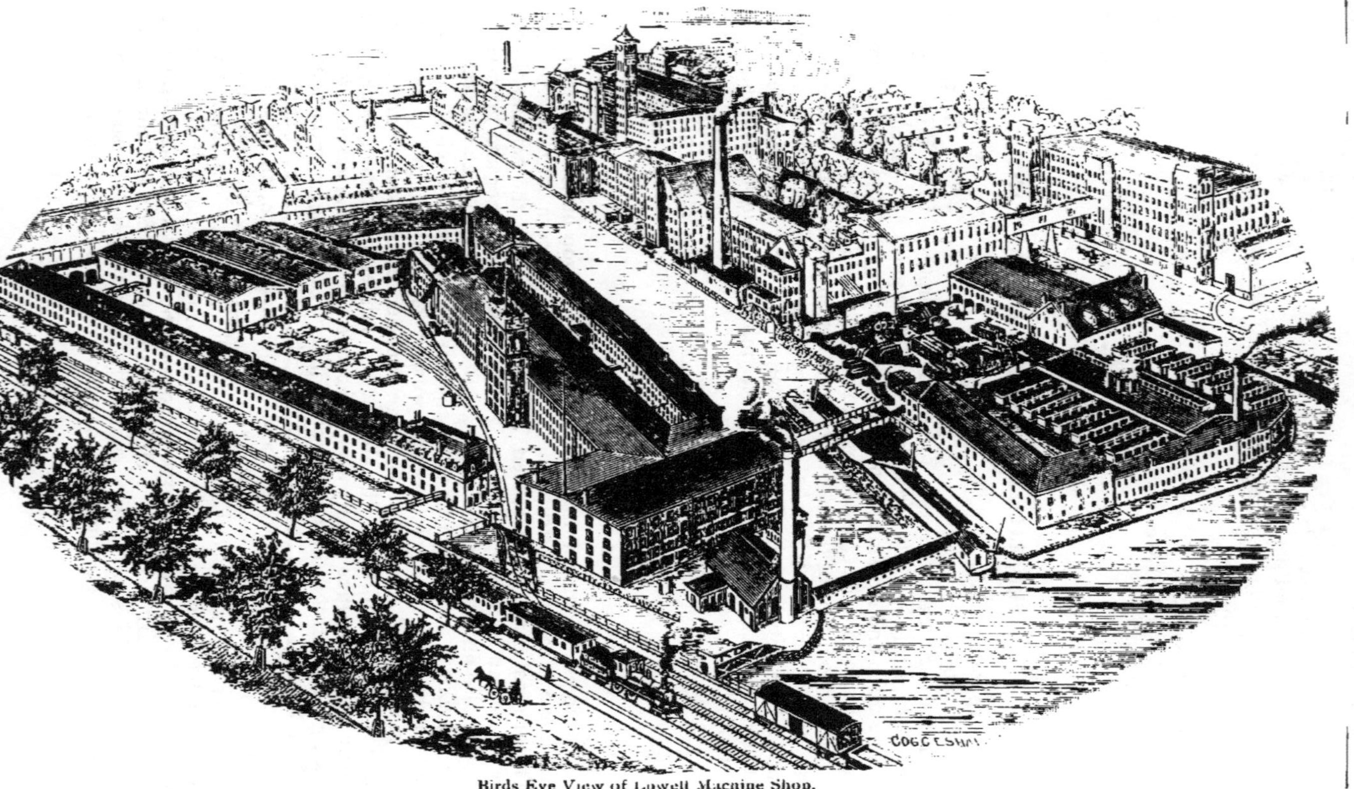

Birds Eye View of Lowell Machine Shop.

LOWELL MACHINE SHOP.

Lowell is not only the home of cotton manufacturing but of cotton and woolen machinery manufacturing. There is no corporation in the city which goes to make up a larger share of the industry in this city than the famous Lowell Machine Shop, which is known the world over as the largest in the world of its kind, making the same machinery. The building of cotton machinery in Lowell was begun by the Merrimack Manufacturing Company, which erected a portion of No. 1 shop in 1824 to furnish their second mill.

It was sold the following year to the proprietors of the Locks & Canals on Merrimack river, a corporation formed to develop the water power and equip mills complete.

This corporation also added to their business the manufacture of locomotives and machinists' tools, and continued in business until 1845, when the whole plant was sold to the Lowell Machine Shop, by whom the business has been carried on uninterruptedly ever since.

The shops are situated between two canals, and have ample railroad facilities, one track running directly into the yards, while there are other tracks on either side.

The entire place, with tenement houses, occupies thirteen acres of land and the floor surface of the present shops, foundry, etc., exceeds seven acres, while the setting up or erecting shops and storage rooms would add nearly as much more; the capacity of the shops has increased more than five times since its establishment. Some two hundred to three hundred men were at first employed, with foundry capacity of one hundred tons of castings per month, while at the present time, fifteen hundred or more men are employed and over seven hundred tons of castings can be produced per month. Many changes have been made in the past few years. Old buildings have been removed and added to, new buildings erected, besides large additions of new special tools, and every exertion possible will be made to execute orders promptly, as well as to maintain the present high standard of work.

MRS. P. H. COREY,

Furniture, Carpets, Stoves, Etc., 192, 194, 196 Middlesex St.

The trade of Lowell, as well as that of the surrounding territories, find that P. H. Corey, 192, 194 and 196 Middlesex street are the people to purchase crockery, piano, jewelry and furniture from, on instalments. From the beginning of the business, which was established about seven years ago, its growth continuing from that day places it second to none in the city of Lowell as an instalment house.

The premises occupied for the business are large and commodious and the stock carried is ample at all times to meet the requirements of the trade, for it can be said they are complete housefurnishers.

The advantages and inducements on the instalment plan are as reasonable as cash terms elsewhere.

The house is conducted on the most modern methods and with its conservative management it can be said that the house is honorable in all its departments and able to meet all requirements in its line. All transactions are based upon the most liberal and fair dealing methods which ave established the reputation of the house.

Interior of Marion's Studio.

MARION, PHOTOGRAPHER.

Corner of Merrimack and Central Sts.

Lowell enjoys the distinction and proud pre-eminence of being the seat of one of the finest artists in photography in the country, who is none other than J. S. Marion, located at the corner of Merrimack and Central Sts. He keeps three upper stories above the handsomely equipped drug store of Ellingwood (a cut of which you will find elsewhere); the opposite page gives but an idea of Mr. Marion's studio and other interesting points.

Mr. Marion was born in Montreal and removed to the city of Lowell at the age of fourteen years, and has resided here ever since. He is about 38 years of age and has been in business for eighteen years. Among the many noted oil paintings, water colors and photographs on exhibition in his reception rooms are those of A. G. Cumnock, Ex-Mayor Pickman, Mayor Courtney, Mr. Fred'k Ayer and many others. A few years ago Mr. Marion took a tour through Europe and while there took lessons of the famous professor of art, Nodar, of Paris. Mr. Marion's studio has unsurpassed facilities as it is conducted under experienced and progressive management. He guarantees satisfaction in every department of art, and prices are always in harmony with skilled labor. In the busy season he gives employment to about seven assistants. A special invitation is given to call and inspect the enormous number of fine works of art which are upon exhibition.

This enterprise is an important one and deserves the high esteem in which it is held by the public of Lowell. "Satisfaction and perfection." is the motto of the work turned out at this house which justly entitles it to the immense success it has achieved in its field of labor.

J. N. CARTER & CO.,

511 Middlesex St.

The well known furnituré house of J. N. Carter & Co. was established Dec. 18, 1885, and has enjoyed a steady increase ever since that date. Mr. Carter is a native of Rutland, Vermont, but has been a resident of Lowell for the past 26 years.

This establishment started in a small store hardly large enough to store a half dozen suits of furniture, but today it occupies a building of sufficient size with a well stocked basement, first and second floors. His line of goods embraces allkinds of house furnishings, such as parlor and chamber suits, crockery, tinware and glassware, The stoves and ranges are those of the new electric make, which took the first premium at the World's Fair. They also handle carpets, oil cloths, mats, curtains, draperies, poles and fixtures, in fact anything in the furniture line can be found at Mr. Carter's establishment. They are also members of the Co-operative Association which loans ten per cent. discount on all purchases at cash prices, and their business is conducted on both a cash and instalment basis. This house has always been very accommodating to the public in general, and no doubt this contributes to their great success. Their prices are right in each and every department and their goods are reliable.

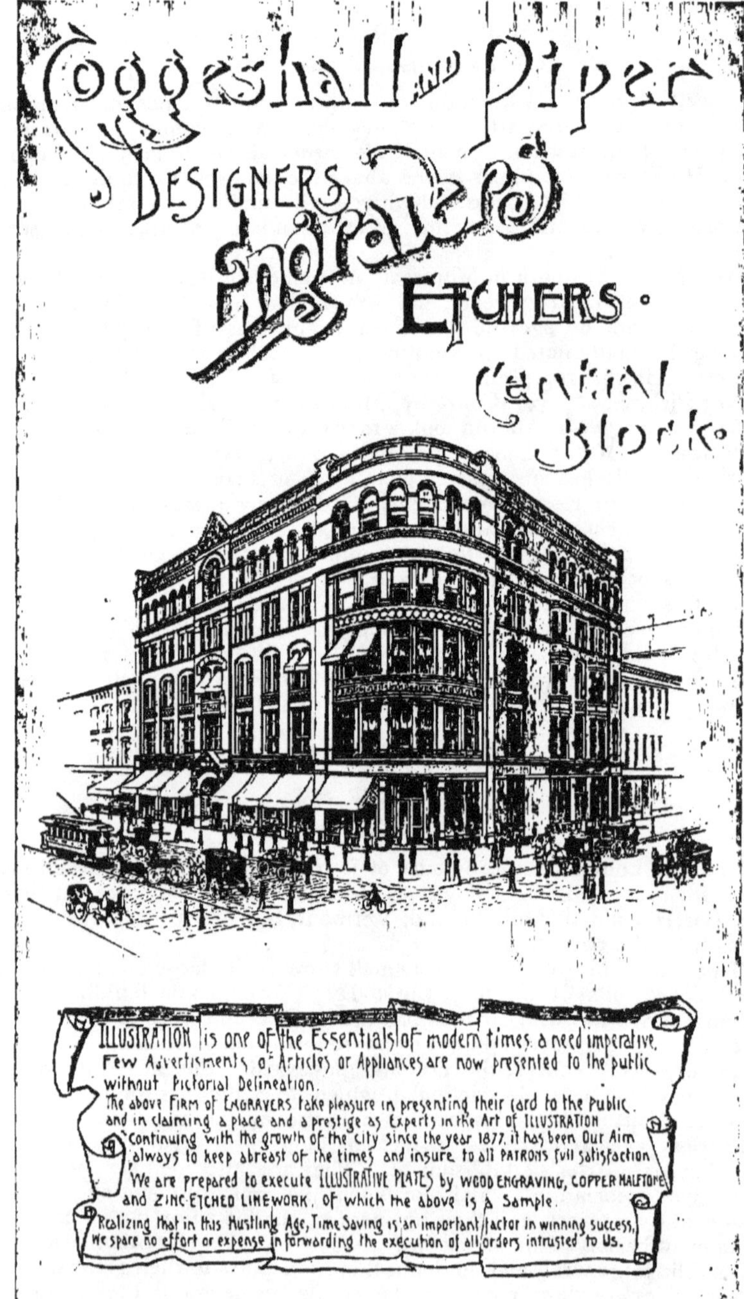
Coggeshall and Piper
Designers
Engravers
Etchers.
Central Block.
ILLUSTRATION is one of the Essentials of modern times a need imperative.
Few Advertisments of Articles or Appliances are now presented to the public without Pictorial Delineation.
The above Firm of ENGRAVERS take pleasure in presenting their card to the Public and in claiming a place and a prestige as Experts in the Art of ILLUSTRATION
Continuing with the growth of the city since the year 1877, it has been Our Aim always to keep abreast of the times and insure to all PATRONS full satisfaction
We are prepared to execute ILLUSTRATIVE PLATES by WOOD ENGRAVING, COPPER HALFTONE and ZINC-ETCHED LINEWORK, of which the above is a Sample.
Realizing that in this Hustling Age, Time Saving is an important factor in winning success, We spare no effort or expense in forwarding the execution of all orders intrusted to Us.

WOODS, SHERWOOD & CO.

572 Bridge St.

Mr. Sherwood was the inventor and patentee of the article first made by this house, and the beautiful, durable and economical, as well as extremely useful, white lustral wire ware, with which the trade and the housekeepers of the country are now familiar, was originated by Mr. Woods, assisted by Mr. Sherwood and others as to particular designs and other details. In 1861 the gentlemen named, formed a co-partnership under the style of Woods, Sherwood & Co., and began manufacturing—at first, of course,—on a limited scale, but increasing facilities and output to keep pace with the demand, which has steadily increased. In 1866 Mr. C. H. Latham, whose name and commercial triumphs had become known in every state of the Union, in Canada, Mexico, South America, Australia and other countries, came to the firm. The works, employing seventy hands, occupy a substantial, modern frame, three-story building at 572 Bridge St., upon which thoroughfare it has a frontage of 45 feet, with a depth of 120 feet. Steam power, steam heat, gaslight and all modern conveniences are provided, while the equipment of ingenious machinery is complete in every department. The product is extremely large, averaging about 60,000 dozen of neat, strong and saleable white lustral twisted wire goods that comprise every article of the kind required in the household, restaurant, office, etc.,—holders, handles, rods, easels, stands, baskets, egg beaters, vegetable boilers, broilers, castors, toilet boxes, traps, brackets, trays, tongs, toy furniture, chains, racks, cases, strainers, dippers, epergnes, forks, gas heaters, gypsy kettles, picture hangers, flower baskets, nut picks, pie racks, plate lifters, potato mashers, toasters, sad iron stands, splasher rods, table mats, tea and coffee balls, pot stands, vases, watch stands, and many other articles; also electroplating of various kinds. Medals and diplomas have been awarded Woods, Sherwood & Co., at the following fairs and expositions held in our own and other countries: Maryland Institute 1867, diploma; Middlesex Mechanics' Asssciation, 1867, silver medal: New Hampshire Mechanics' and Art Association, 1868, gold medal; Massachusetts Charitable Mechanics' Association, 1869, bronze medal; New England Agricultural Society, 1871, first premium, silver medal; New England Agricultural Society, 1872, first premium, silver medal; Cincinnatti Industrial Exposition, 1872 and 1873, first premium, silver medal; Massachusetts Charitable Mechanics' Association, 1874, diploma; International Exhibition of Chili, 1875, bronze medal; Centennial International Exhibition, Philadelphia, 1876, bronze medal; Massachusetts Charitable Mechanics' Association, 1878, bronze medal; International Exhibition, Sidney, N. S. W., 1879, first premium, bronze medal;

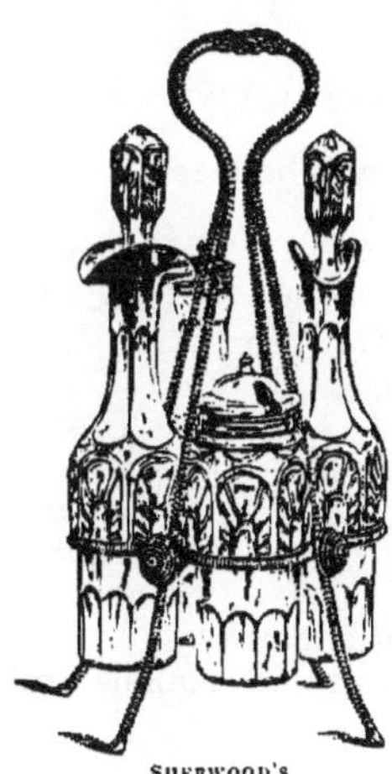

SHERWOOD'S

World's Industrial and Cotton Centennial Exposition, New Orleans 1884-5, bronze medal; North, Central and South America Exposition, New Orleans, 1885-6, bronze medal; Columbian Exhibition, Chicago, Ill., 1893, gold medal.

MIDDLESEX COMPANY.

Incorporated 1830.
Present capital, - - - - - - $750,000.

DIRECTORS, 1893.

Arthur T. Lyman, Robert H. Gardiner, M. R. Wendell, Augustus Lowell, Geo. Z. Silsbee; Charles P. Curtis, president; O. H. Perry, treasurer.

The goods manufactured are indigo blue coatings, cassimeres, police, yacht and cadet cloths, ladies' sackings and beavers. 20,000 pounds of clean wool are consumed per week, and 12,500 6-4 yards of cloth made. The mills are located at the junction of the Pawtucket canal and Concord river, with Warren St. as the southwesterly boundary line. The company owns nearly seven and a half acres of land.

MASSACHUSETTS COTTON MILLS.

Incorporated 1839.

Officers: W. E. Southworth, agent; J. C. Wadleigh, supt.; E. G. Childs, asst. supt.; David Healy, Jr., paymaster.

Located at junction of Merrimack and Concord rivers, between Bridge and Merrimack Sts.

Capital, - - - - - - - - $1,800,000.

Charles L. Lovering, treasurer, Boston. Smith, Hogg & Gardner, selling agents, 66 Chauncy St., Boston, and 115 & 117 Worth St., New York.

Spindles, - - - - - - - 127,000. Looms, - - - - - - - 4,061.
Females employed, - - - 1,300. Males employed, - - - 600.
Yards made per week, - - - - 1.000,000.
Pounds of cotton consumed per week. - - - - 300,000.
Floor area of mills, - - - - - - 19 acres.
Power 3,000 horse-power of water wheels; 3,000 of engines.
Kind of goods made: sheetings, shirtings, drillings, canton flannels and denims.

DIRECTORS, 1893.

Arthur T. Lyman, Frederick F. Ayer, Jas. C. Ayer, Harrison Gardner.

Annual meeting, last Tuesday in March.

No. of mills, - - - - - - - - 6. Spindles, - - - - 118,000.
Looms, - - - - - - - - - - 4,050. Females employed, 1,600.
Males employed, - - - - - - 600. Yards made per week, 700,000.
Pounds cotton used per week, - - - - - 240,00.
Kind of goods made: cotton flannels, drillings, dress goods, fancy shirtings.

Tons coal per year, - - - - 9,000. Gallons oil per year, - 12,000.
Pounds starch per year, - 150,000. Water wheels, 11 Turbines; 4-8 Ft., & 6-4 Ft., in diameter.
Steam power, . - - 7 engines, 2100 horse-power.

LOWELL EDUCATIONAL AND INDUSTRIAL UNION,

228 Worthen St.

The members of the Women's Educational and Industrial Union respectfully invite you to join this association, formed for social and intellectual enjoyment. The only by-law is, "Do unto others as ye would that others do unto you."

The regular sessions are Tuesdays of each week, at 3 p. m., except on Club Tea days, when the meetings are appointed an hour later. A general invitation is extended to all to write essays, or give talks on any subject in which they are interested, yet no one is obliged to take part in the exercises. Listeners are as welcome as speakers, yet it is hoped that each one will be inclined to give as well as receive information. The industrial department has constantly on hand a fine grade of useful and ornamental articles, the handiwork of members of the association, for the sale of which ten per cent. commission is charged. This enables many to obtain money for charitable or other purposes. Orders will be received and promptly executed for knitting, crocheting, embroidering and all kinds of plain and fancy needlework; for painting in oil, or water colors, on canvas, cloth, silk, wood or iron.

In the food department a good assortment of cake, cookies and salad dressing is always on hand. Home made bread and rolls made to order. Wedding cake is a specialty and made on due notice. Cold ham constantly on sale by slice or pound. Dinners and lunches served after 11.30 a. m. Ice cream constantly on hand; sherbets made to order.

In addition to the above there is a private school connected, which is conducted with the greatest success by Miss L. A. Hill.

HAMILTON MANUFACTURING CO.

Incorporated 1825.
Present capital - - - - - $1,800,000
Officers, with date of appointment.

TREASURERS.

William Appleton,	March 5, 1825.	Ebenezer Appleton,	Feb. 3, 1830.
George W. Lyman,	June 1, 1833.	Thomas G. Cary,	June 4, 1839.
William B. Bacon,	July 22, 1859.	Arthur T. Lyman,	Dec. 19, 1860.
Arthur L. Devens,	June 30, 1863.	Eben Bacon, -	June 27, 1867.
Samuel Batchelder,	Nov. 19, 1869.	Geo. R. Chapman,	Jan. 18, 1870.
Jas. A. Dupee, - - - -	1870.	Died, - - - -	Oct. 18, 1886.
James Longley, -	Oct. 19, 1886.	Chas. B. Amory,	Nov. 15, 1886.

SUPERINTENDENTS.

Samuel Batchelder, - - -	1825.	O. H. Moulton, - - -	1864.
John Avery, - - - - - -	1831.		

Talbot Memorial Hall, Billerica.

Moody School.

Oaklands.

ASSISTANT SUPERINTENDENT OF PRINT WORKS.

William Spencer, - - - - 1828. William Harley, - - - - 1866.
William Hunter, - - - - 1862. Thomas Walsh, - - - - 1876.

ASSISTANT SUPERINTENDENT OF COTTON DEPARTMENT

Ferdinand Rodliff.

DIRECTORS, 1893.

Thomas Wigglesworth, James Longley, Charles Henry Parker, Henry S. Grew, Edward I. Browne, J. Herbert Sawyer, Charles Amory.

James Longley, President, Charles B. Amory, Treasurer, Frederick W. Way, Clerk.

Annual meeting, second Thursday in July.

No. Mills, - 6 and Print Works. Spindles, - - - - 109,816
Looms, - - - - - - - 3,035. Females employed, - - 1,200.
Males employed, - - - 800. Yards made per week, 730,000.
Pounds cotton used per week, 180,000. Yards dyed and printed per week, - - - - 720,000

Kind of goods made:—flannels, prints, ticks, stripes, drills and shirtings, 5 to 37.

Tons coal per year, - - 11,000. Bushels charcoal per year, 300.
Cords wood per year, - - 200. Gallons oil per year, - 11,000
Pounds starch per year, - 450,000. Drugs and dye stuffs, amount per year, - - - 250,000

Ten turbine and forty-one engines of 2600 horse-power, including small engines used for printing machines, furnish the motive power of this company. The plant includes about seven and one-half acres of land.

THE PROPRIETORS OF LOCKS & CANALS.

Incorporated 1792, Capital, $600,000.

Officers, with date of appointment.

TREASURERS.

Joseph Cutler, - - - - 1792. W. W. Prout, - - - - 1804.
Samuel Cutler, - - - - 1809. Samuel Tenney, - - - 1817.

SPECIAL AGENTS.

William Boott, - - - - 1838. James B. Francis, - - 1845.
James Francis, - - - - 1885.

ENGINEERS.

Paul Moody, - - - - - - 1824. Joel Lewis, - - - - 1826.
George W. Whistler, - - 1834. James Francis, . - - 1837.
James Francis, - - - - 1885.

CONSULTING ENGINEERS.

James B. Francis, - 1885, 1892. Hiram F. Mills, - - - 1893.

TREASURERS AND AGENTS.

Kirk Boott, - - - - - - 1822. Joseph Tilden, - - - 1837.

TREASURERS.

P. T. Jackson, - - - - - 1838. John T. Morse, - - - 1845.

DIRECTORS, 1893.

Lucius M. Sargent, President. Howard Stockton, Louis Robeson, O. H. Perry, Eliot C. Clarke, John T. Morse, Treasurer, Charles B. Amory, Arthur T. Lyman, Alphonso S. Covel, Charles L. Lovering, Robert H. Stevenson.

Annual meeting, third Tuesday of September.

F. B. HILL & CO.

348 to 352 Middlesex St.

The above firm have recently moved from their shop on Revere St., to the old stand of G. F. Hill on Middlesex St. which was established 30 years ago by Mr. Hill, Jr., who has made a reputation for good work that the new firm will continue to maintain. This firm does carriage repairing in all its branches and employs from 10 to 14 men. This firm does not build any buggies but does build a first-class business wagon in any style or shape, and repairs anything that runs on wheels, and does it in first class shape.

HILDRETH BUILDING.

The Hildreth Building is the most prominent building in the city of Lowell. It is owned and conducted by Thomas Nesmith. The prominent tenants of the building are as follows:

Dr. Huntoon, Room 37; Metropolitan Stock Exchange, G. M. Milmore, Gen. Mgr., Room 1; Young's Hair Dressing establishment, Rooms 8 and 9; A. S. Taylor, Wholesale Watch Dealer and Diamond Broker, Room 2; W. D. Brown, Real Estate and Mutual Life Insurance, Room 2; Charles Kelley & Co., Real Estate, Room 2; M. G. Leonard, the Tenant Agent, Room 5; J. F. Haskell, Attorney-at-law, Room 5; George L. Hubbard, Real Estate, Room 6; Hall & Mayotte, Merchant Tailors Rooms 34 and 35; G. Staynor & Co., Bankers and Brokers, Room 33; Walter E. Stratton, Banjo and Guitar Teacher, Room 36; J. F. Corbett, Attorney-at-law, Room 39; W. S. Marshall, Attorney-at-law, room 39 J. S. Burke, Attorney-at-law, Room 39; C. F. Foss, Contractors and Builders, Room 14; Walter Leighton, Real Estate and Attorney-at-law, Room 13: J. S. Murphy, Attorney-at-law, Room 34; H. A. Brown, Attorney-at-law, Room 21; W. H. Bent, Attorney-at-law, Room 21; Solon W. Stevens, Attorney-at-law, Room 21; D. E. Dudley, Room 21; Mutual Benefit Life Insurance, Room 21; A. G. Lamson, Attorney-at-law, Room 20; Prentiss Webster, Attorney-at-law, Room 20; Davis & Raynes, Architect, Room 49; F. H. Pearson, Attorney-at-law, Room

44; J. A. Gately, Attorney-at-law, Room 44; N. D. Pratt, Notary Public and Attorney-at-law, Room 45; Thomas Nesmith, owner of Hildreth Building, Room 38; J. F. Owens, Attorney-at-law, Room 17; J. A. Maguire, Attorney-at-law, Room 18; J. H. Morrison, Attorney-at-law, Room 11; Smith & Brooks, Civil Engineers, Room 26; Freeman, Photographer, open Monday and Saturday evenings, Rooms 52, 53, and 54; Stickney & Austin, Architects, Rooms, 28, 50, 51; Isaac Pitman School of Shorthand, Room 31; W. H. Emery, Room 29, A; G. W. Poor, Notary Public and Attorney-at-law, Room 29; C. S. Lilley, Attorney-at-law, Room 29 and F. E. Dunbar, Attorney-at-law, Room 29.

MME. C. L. GREGOIRE,

318 and 320 Merrimack St,

The establishment of Mme. C. L. Gregoire is without doubt the most elegant millinery establishment in the city of Lowell. It has long been the leading one, the interior being of the most attractive style, where imported and domestic designs of millinery are shown. Without a doubt their style of decorating and trimming their windows is far superior to any other in the city, and few millinery establishments in any city of the United States have a more attractive front, in which is displayed at different times perfect wax figures, with all the hues and coloring of the human face, adding greatly to the elegance ot finely made millinery.

The windows are arched with incandescent lights, the rear being upholstered in fine silk, with draperies of tinseled curtains and mirrors. It is not because the prices are exorbitant that the place is made so attractive, but the public having past relations are in a position to know that prices at this leading millinery establishment are always in harmony with quality. The proprietor gives it her personal attention and dictates every detail, to which the immense success is attributed. Their motto is "satisfaction guaranteed."

W. F. TRUMBELL,

Pianos and Organs.

Wells F. Trumbell was born in Hill, N. H., Feb. 13th, 1857. His folks soon after came to this city where he attended the public schools until at the age of sixteen he left for Boston, where he pursued the study of music and pianoforte tuning. Returning to this city he soon won for himself a reputation as a teacher and pianoforte turner. For the past ten years he has been better known to the public as a tuner and dealer in pianos and organs. He has handled nearly all of the first class makes of pianos, including the "Crown," "Chickering," "New England," etc.

His close attention to business, together with fair dealings, and extremely low prices has won for him a reputation which no competition can ever wreck.

J. C. DONOVAN.

Horse Furnishings and Carriage Goods, Ware Rooms, 57 Market Street.

The above establishment goes to make up the principal industry of its kind in this city. It occupies the three story brick building known as the Brabrook Block. J. A. Brabrook conducted business as a harness

manufacturer at this stand for over 50 years. The present proprietor, J. C. Donovan started in a small way and by thrift and close application to business has built up a trade that extends to all parts of New England. In the manufacture of harness he has a large force of practical harness-makers, whose skill is unsurpassed. They turn out the "Ideal Express Harness" which has no equal, and in fact harnesses of every description, which are all handmade and excelled by none.

Aside from the manufacture, he has a repair department where everything in the line receives careful attention. Also two floors which are fitted up as salesrooms, the first floor covering a large area and containing horse furnishings, carriage and turf goods of foreign and domestic manufacture. This firm is also agent for Champion Bolles Spreaders.

On the second floor you can see and examine over two hundred harnesses which are all of modern make, made from the best stock that can be secured. Everything is sold with a guarantee. It is also agent for the "Darr Two Minute Harness," which is the only practical harness for track use. It enables the horse to trot much faster than with the ordinary harness.

An establishment of this kind adds much to the prosperity of a city because if a corporation or individual knows that their wants are within their midst they are at ease. This is the long felt want that J. C. Donovan fills. He makes a study of the horse and no matter how small the margin may be on this necessity, it is his object to have it in stock in order to have his line complete. He is a well satisfied man when his patrons find what they want at this establishment.

DR. W. H. DOWNS,

Surgeon Dentist, 243 Central St.

Dr. Downs is a native of New Haven, Conn., a graduate of Prof. Fabrique's Scientific Academy and also the School of Arts under Prof. Flagg. He removed to Lowell opening Dental parlors in 1873 and has followed his profession ever since. He is prominent in many secret and social organizations and clubs, two of which he organized. He was pronounced an expert at a Dental Clinic in Connecticut a few years ago upon extracting before the fraternity, among them the late Dr. Tasher of Boston. Demonstrating with the anaesthetic nitrous oxide gas, administering, unassisted, with the aid of his inventions, the nitrous oxide stand which is so much in use and salable all over the United States, Canada and England, together with other useful inventions to the profession.

H. L. MILLS,

Bicycles, Tool Sharpening and Repair Shop.

This place was established in 1883 at No. 475 Broadway, the proprietor of which is Mr. H. L. Mills, a practical mechanic, who is daily earning a reputation for himself in fine repair work of every description especially bicycle repairing; his line also consists of bicycle attachments such as tires, bells, pulleys, wheels, brakes, and handles.

Mr. Mills is a native of Maine and has been a resident of Lowell for about twelve years. He is also agent for the Liberty, Niagara and Demorest bicycles of which he has a number and has modern facilities for the repairing of the same. The floorage is about 20 x 45 feet. Mr. Mills is a congenial and progressive business man and assures satisfaction to all of his patrons.

LOWELL STEAM CARPET CLEANING WORKS.

The well known Lowell Steam Carpet Cleaning Works is one point of great interest in the line of industry in the city of Lowell, the proprietor of which is G. Maddock, who is a native of Lowell and began business in the smallest way imaginable, until today it is an immense enterprise. The works were established in 1884 at 42 Weed street. As you enter the office door, at the right is located the office; directly opposite is a

moth proof storage room for carpets; in the rear of the office is a large room about 32 feet square, where upholstered work is set up when finished, and in the rear of this room is located his engine room, in which is a 20 horse-power engine, which drives a large thrashing or carpet machine making 160 revolutions a minute. Directly at one side of the room is located a large fan which sucks up the dust and dirt from the machine while in operation. In the rear of the carpet machine is located the feather room for the renovation of feather beds, etc. The carpet sewing department, which is at the left, is a large commodious room. At the right of this building is a large storehouse in which goods are stored for a short length of time. No doubt their process of removing buffalo bugs and all kinds of insects is the most proficient method in use, and without a doubt the factory is one of the cleanest in the United States. Invitations are extended to the public to inspect this work at all times, when Mr. Maddocks will be pleased to show you through or have his assistants do so.

The size of the building is 160 x 32 feet, and every department with details is carried on in the most thorough manner, "up-to-date" principles only being in use in cleaning and disinfecting. Carpets and rugs of all kinds taken up, steamed and cleaned properly and thoroughly.

They also make a specialty of making, laying, fitting and repairing carpets, and hair mattresses and feather beds are renovated by steam ; also furniture upholstering and naphtha renovating. This house is one of the fast growing factories in the city of Lowell, and the unanimous support of the public has only been obtained by square, upright, honest dealings, which have given weight and prominence to this house. Goods are called for and delivered.

ESTEY PIANO CO.,

Main Offices Southern Boulevard, Near Harlem Bridge, N. Y., Lowell Office, Merrimack St.

In every civilized country on the globe the name of Estey is a household word with lovers of music. It is a guarantee for that exquisite quality of tone in musical instruments that commands confidence, admiration and enthusiasm.

FACTORY BUILT 1885, DOUBLED 1890.

The factory recently erected is one of the best arranged and most magnificent on the globe, proof of which is that four factories have been built practically after its model. The system of manufacture is the most thoroughly scientific to be found among modern establishments. The most artistic designs, made by leading artists of America, always keeping pace with the changes of style ; the Estey is a recognized leader in this respect. New construction of frame, by means of which the strain is made independent of the case, and the exquisite quality of tone maintained and enriched ; cases constructed on the built-up system of quarter sawed lumber, double crossbanded, quadruple veneered (excepting ebonized cases, which are hard maple), avoiding the defects to a most astonishing degree which have been the bane of all pianos : new system of sextuple veneering of quarter sawed old growth iron maple, the best system yet invented, rivaling all others in strength and durability, dropping down so as to place the music at the proper height and in the right position. There is no possibility of the music being torn, as it rests in an easy position. New and perfected scale for each style, superior to any heretofore introduced.

The dealers who handle these pianos and purchasers of them not only endorse the foregoing statements, but bear witness to the entire satisfaction which these instruments are giving.

Associate Building.

MERRIMACK CLOTHING CO.,

Merrimack St., Cor Worthen.

Probably no better illustration of public appreciation of uniform perfection and practical advantage can be cited than the phenomenal popularity of the celebrated Merrimack Clothing company, situated at Monument Square, directly opposite City Hall, in one of the finest buildings, (a cut of which is on the opposite page) in the city of Lowell, and whose goods are everywhere recognized as the highest standard of quality and reliability. This, too, has not been the result of skilful advertising. It has been brought about by the unremitting aim of the firm to deserve the favor of customers by selling the best line of goods from the best manufacturers, of the finest quality in weights and shades of clothing, with prices in keeping with quality.

This house has not only a beautiful location but the interior is of the finest type, it having a large clothing department, hats, caps, and gent's furnishings. This establishment was oganized Aug. 1, 1893. The officers are: Miles F. Brennan, president; H. O'Sullivan, treasurer; P. O'Hearn, P. Keyes, Robert J. Butcher, James J. Coffey, James O'Sullivan, directors; John A. O'Hearn, manager. Capital invested $50,-000. These are some of the most progressive and enterprising citizens of Lowell and the splendid success they have achieved is as pronounced as it is gratifying.

THE CRYSTAL,

Associate Building, Worthen St.

The Crystal is the name of the most elegant saloon in the city, The equipments embrace a handsome plate front of about 40 feet with a depth of 100 feet, with a high studding. At the right of the entrance will be noticed a fine office of quartered oak, with beveled plate windows in it. Right beyond the office is located a handsome bar at the rear of which is a French plate mirror handsomely covered with fine screening draped in various shades. Directly opposite is the finely located lunch counter and in the rear of that is a most complete grill room.

No pains or money have been spared to make this a most elegant saloon, it having electric lights and fans and having gas connection in cases of emergency.

MR. C. M. YOUNG.,

Undertaker, Prescott Street.

One of the most prominent undertakers, outside of Boston in northern Massachusetts, and one most prominently connected with public interest and long residence in the city of Lowell is C. M. Young, who is established on Prescott St. The establishment is fitted up with antique furniture, with closed casket and receivers. He has a very attractive location and has the best accommodations in hearse and funeral supplies in Lowell, gaining reputation by efficient work. He is a native of Lowell and has figured as a business man and a representative of his line for many years. His attendants are all most agreeable and are responsible in the discharge of duties, and with Mr. C. M. Young's personal attention satisfaction is guaranteed. Office connected with telephone.

GREENWOOD BROS.,

Groceries, Boots, Shoes and Real Estate.

The house of Greenwood Bros. is well known in the city of Lowell, having been established in 1865, and ever since its birth it has steadily grown so that it at present occupies a building three stories and a half high, with a frontage of 44 feet and a depth of 80 feet, in a very substantial location. Messrs. Greenwood are both natives of Haverhill, Mass., and when they located in Lowell, started in a very small way. They thus continued business for a short time when they found that their business needed more substantial premises and decided to enlarge their building until at present they have displayed many goods. On the ground floor is a commodious office connected with a well assorted grocery department; to the right, is located the boot and shoe department; the balance of the upper story and rear are used for storage.

The members of the firm are O. O. and M. Greenwood, both of them being progressive business men, and it can be said that their success in business is attributed to straightforward, honest dealings. Relations with this firm will confirm this belief, They are the publishers of what is known as "Greenwood Bros.' Monthly Courier" which publishes facts relating to their lively nature in business relations.

ADELAIDE E. NOYES.

Graduate of the Emerson College of Oratory, Boston. Elocution, voices and physical culture.

Fancy rythmic movements, adapted to cultivate easy and graceful motions of the body, and to develop correct carriage and overcome physical defects, such as tendencies to crooked limbs, "toe in" walk, inclined or round shoulders, hollow chest, etc.

The voice will also receive attentton with the idea of teaching correct breathing, articulation and pronounciation, with special care given to impediments or defects in speech, such as stammering, hesitation, weak voice, etc.

Special attention is given to children, the child being taught to express ideas, not merely to repeat words.

Rooms open Sept. 18, at 23 Swan Block, Central St., Lowell.

MCKISSOCK & PACKER.

Steam Carpet Cleaning Company, 60 Plain St.

The well-known house of McKissock & Packer, Steam Carpet Cleaning Company, was established in 1887 by Mr. McKissock. The business continued under that head until 1894, at which time Mr. J. Packer was admitted to partnership, At that time they put in new carpet cleaning machines which have run steadily to do all kinds of work in a thorough manner and at short notice. All work is done indoors which enables them to work in all kinds of weather, and if you are contemplating moving they will take up your carpets, clean them, and make them over to fit your new house. The past few years' growth of this house has been astonishing. They have commodious quarters at 60 Plain St., where the work in various departments is carried on. They make a specialty of cutting and laying new carpets, also all kinds of upholstering and renovating feather beds, hair mattresses, etc. Goods are called for and delivered.

CHARLES ALBERT EASTMAN, A. B., M. D.

Dr. Charles A. Eastman, son of Dr. Joseph H. and Eliza J. (Bunker) Eastman, whose maternal grandfather, John K. Bunker served in the war of 1812, was born in Fryeburg, Oxford County, Maine, April 6th, 1851. After a thorough education in the classical branches, he began the study of medicine, never neglecting, however, the natural sciences, for which he had a special predilection. He began his medical studies in 1870 at the Geneva Medical College, New York, where he was graduated with honors. Impelled by his natural taste for medical science, he matriculated in the medical department of the University of Baltimore in 1891 for the purpose of pursuing advanced studies in Surgery and Bacterioscopy, completing the course and graduating in 1893.

He also pursued a successful post-graduate course and passed for the degree of M. D., at the Boston University School of Medicine.

Dr. Eastman has not only been actively engaged as a practitioner of medicine and surgery for the past twenty-two years, but he has devoted himself largely to the promotion of educational work in his native state, having served on the Boards of Education and as supervisor of the public schools. Dr. Eastman is also a member of the Massachusetts Medical Society, Boston Gynaecological Society, ex-member of the American Medical Association, member of the Boston Surgical and Obstetrical Society, and also served as superintendent and surgeon-in-chief to the Middletown hospital for two years. He is a prominent member of the I. O. O. F. in the Lodge, Encampment and Canton branch of the order, and was surgeon-general in the department of the East with the rank of Lieut. Col. for three years. He is an active member of the A. O. U. W., Royal Arcanum and other secret societies; is a member ot the Sons of Maine, the First Congregational church. Lowell, and is examiner for several leading Life Insurance companies.

His original researches include abdominal, plastic and obstetrical surgery. In operations his methods for operation for hernial conditions, piles, rectum and bladder have been most successful and received high commendation.

Faulkner's Mills, North Billerica. Abbott's Mills, Forge Village.

ABBOTT & CO ,

Graniteville and Forge Village.

This extensive enterprise has long been one of the greatest of Massachusetts industries. The business was established in 1855 by Messrs. John W. Abbott, J. W. Abbott Jr., and G. Sargent. Two years later the interests of the two last named were purchased by Allan Cameron, and in 1876 Abiel Abbott was admitted to an interest in the business under the firm name of Abbott & Co., being Allan Cameron, John W. and Abiel J. Abbott. The mills of the firm are located at Graniteville and Forge Village, in the town of Westford.

FAULKNER MANUFACTURING CO.

Established 1811 . . . . Incorporated 1880.

Geo. M. Preston, president and treasurer, Boston.

W. A. Evans, Agent.

WOOLEN MANUFACTURERS.

Make all-wool Flannels and Dress Goods.
Run eight sets of Cards and 58 Broad Looms.
Engine, 120 horse-power.
Employ about 95 hands, pay Fridays.
Selling Agents: Faulkner, Page & Co., Boston and New York.

MOIR BROTHERS & CO.,

Merrimack St.

The enterprise of Moir Brothers & Co. was established in 1891 and has since built up a trade that places it in the front rank of its kind in Lowell. The premises occupied for the business comprise a front of about 30 feet and a depth of about 70 feet. The left-hand half of the store is devoted solely to a handsomely arranged millinery department which is trimmed in the various seasons with all the modern "up-to-date" styles with prices in keeping with quality. Their line also embraces fancy goods, hose, underwear, gloves, dress trimmings, small ware, laces, ribbons, corsets, cotton underwear, jewelry, wrappers, yarns and fancy goods; while the store is largely devoted to French millinery, the rest of the goods are in harmony with the style; about 30 ladies are in attendance in the busy season, several being efficient masters of the French language.

Mr. George Moir, the manager and one of the proprietors, is a native of Scotland, and has been a resident of Lowell for the past 20 years. Previous to starting in business he filled a position at F. G. Mitchell & Co.'s store in which he had charge of several departments. The reputation of this house in the past four years has only been established by selling goods at prices extremely low, and offering advantages to the public which catch the eye; enjoying close relations with importers, manufacturers, etc, enables this house to furnish the trade with goods in their line at extremely reasonable prices.

D. L. PAGE CO.,

Confectioners and Caterers.

We do not think that in regard to the second division of our class, viz: confectionery, our task is a trivial one. At the risk of being considered fanciful, or high flown—we hold that confectionery may be regarded as the poetic principle, applied to the very matter ot common food. We are deeply persuaded, too, that children's happy faces and gleeful laughter, are much more of a power in the weary world than dreamed of in most people's philosophy, and from the time whereof the memory of man run-

neth not to the contrary, cakes and lolly pops have been inseparably associated with juvenial bliss. We, therefore, very readily come to the conclusion that philosophy may find as much to command in beautiful and wholesome confectionery, as in the "steamboat, the railway, in the thoughts that shake mankind."

"With perfect unanimity we have awarded to D. L. Page, Lowell, Mass., for confectionery of singular excellence, a silver medal."

FREDERICK T. GREENHALGE, Chairman of Judges.

MR. GEO. V. GREGG.,

Merchant Tailor, Central St.

Of importance to the male sex is the establishment of the responsible, experienced, popular merchant tailor, Mr. G V. Gregg, who is established on Central St., at the junction of Prescott. Mr. Gregg has the reputation of knowing how to fit forms perfectly. He is also noted for carrying fabrics of all styles and weaves such as tweeds, woolens, worsteds, etc., which greatly go to make up the value in dealing with a responsible house. His prices are always in harmony with quality, workmanship and trimming, to which Mr. Gregg gives his personal attention in the turning out of his product. Mr. Gregg is closely identified with the commercial interest and welfare of the city. His past success is only attributed to fair, square and honest dealings, which have gained for him this reputation. He is one of Lowell's broad guage business men and fast climbing the ladder to success. Business relations with this house will prove of the most advantageous kind. His enterprise has proven a valuable factor to the resources of Lowell.

C. H. HANSON & CO.,

Rock St.

One of the oldest and most reliable horse and carriage marts is the well-known establishment of C. H. Hanson & Co., which is located at 39 and 45 Rock St It was originally established in 1864, and its reputation ever since its birth has grown famous in the handling of horses and carriages in the Merrimack Valley. They make a specialty of road and draft horses, carriages, harnesses, and horse furnishing, storage for carriages, etc. Their premises are large and spacious which, with their storehouses, sheds and adjoining stables easily cover an acre of ground. Every Thursday morning at 10 a. m. there is conducted an auction sale of native and western horses.

Mr. Hanson is a progressive and enterprising man and an esteemed citizen, and the important house he is now conducting has long been one of the chief factors of its line and has helped to develop the enterprise and push of our noble city. Public sentiment endorses reliable and honorable dealings, and to this only is attributed the great success of this enterprise.

BOARD OF TRADE CIGAR.

The well known Board of Trade Cigar is manufactured by W. P. Gordon, who is located in the Marston Building, No. 4 and 6 Marston street. This is a cigar which pleases the most select smokers; a ten cent cigar with a ten cent smoke in value. Try them and be convinced. This is the building which they are manufactured in.

THE MARSTON BUILDING

Middlesex and Marston Sts.

One of Lowell's live and energetic business men is Mr. George H. Marston. He is a gentleman widely known by his connections with the book, stationery and paper trade of Lowell. He was associated with Mr. George Prince under the firm name of Marston & Prince, during a long business career. Mr. Marston has acquired considerable real estate in various sections of the city. A few years ago Mr. Marston retired from the above mentioned firm and devoted most of his time to the care of his property. In 1889, when the Appleton Company disposed of part of their boarding house property on Middlesex St., Mr. Marston was the first purchaser of one of the lots on which now stands the widely-known Marston building, located on the corner of Middlesex and Marston Sts. The lower floor is occupied by extract manufacturers, confectionery stores, and the well-known "Board of Trade" Cigar is manufactured in this building. No building has a finer construction and neater in appearance than this which is of brick with granite trimmings, tastefully relieved by modest designs in artistic terra cotta works. He has one son, Joseph N., who is medical student at Harvard College. Mr. Marston, with his usual enterprise, was the first to improve the Appleton property. He is the possessor of a fine residence surrounded by elegant grounds in Centralville, also of other valuable real estate in this and sister cities. This building has added greatly to the location in which it is situated, and since the location of the new postoffice it has become the most valuable business site on Middlesex St.

CHARLES F. STOTT,

Flat-Iron Building, Highlands.

A leading exponent of the progress in retail business on the Highlands is Charles F. Stott, who is a native of Lowell, and has been located at the above place for the past six years, having established his business in 1889 in the market and provision business. He controls a great amount of the Highland trade and can be thoroughly relied upon in every particular.

He has vegetables in and out of season and fine delicacies in fruit can be found there at all times. He has telephone connection; has double entrances, both Westford and Pine Sts., and a frontage of about 30 feet, certainly the most convenient quarters for his line of business in the Highlands. Mr. Stott's establishment requires the assistance of five hands and three delivery wagons, making the best possible facilities for receiving and delivering orders.

MASTER BUILDERS' EXCHANGE.

This Exchange is known as the Master Builders' Exchange of the City of Lowell.

The purpose of this Exchange is declared to be the establishment of an Exchange composed of Master Mechanics in the various branches of constructive work used in the erection of buildings, and the maintenance of reading and exchange rooms for the accommodation of the said Exchange, affording facilities for information, and the interchange and discussion of social, architectural and business matters. Its purpose is also declared to be the placing of the Exchange on a responsible basis by creating a yearly assessment, payable in advance, that the Exchange may be a body responsible to those with whom it may have dealings.

The special aims ot the Exchange are declared to be :—

First. The establishment of a certain standard of worth and excellence, which shall be a perquisite for admission to membership, to the end that membership in the Exchange may be a reasonable assurance to the public of skill, honorable reputation, and probity.

Second. The defence and security of the best interests of mechanics in the building trades, by providing means and authority, whereby members of the Exchange may demand and secure honorable dealing among themselves and in their relations to others.

Third. The attainment of uniformity of action among the individuals forming the Exchange, upon the general principles set forth, and upon such special principles as may be from time to time decided upon as best for the good of all concerned.

E. H. MORSE.

Carriages of All Grades. 139 Middle St.

This leading and representative firm is composed solely of E. H. Morse. who is a direct successor of the entire premises formerly occupied by the Sawyer Carriage Company. Mr. Morse has handled carriages of all grades and styles for the past three years at the above location, where he has managed and carried on a successful business since 1892. Much of the business is done by orders received through the mail direct from customers and all are satisfactorily filled. The premises occupied is a large and substantial four-story building having a good amount of floorage room.

The stock handled comprises every known make of carriages, carts, wagons, surries, traps, Goddards, etc. Fair and liberal treatment are among the many advantages offered to the trade by this firm. Mr. Morse is a man of public spirit well adapted to fill the responsible position in every particular. His business interests are not only in Lowell but he has a branch in Nashua and several other places throughout the state.

McQUADE & CO.,

Constables.

The establishment of McQuade & Co. was founded in 1893 by John A. McQuade. Three years previous to that time he was in the employ of J. B. Swift, but in 1893 he decided that his large acquaintance among the commercial houses of Lowell warranted a start for himself, which he did in a small way laboring under every inconvenience. He has been a constable since 1890, appointed by Charles D. Palmer, and also carries on an auctioneer business. He is associate detective for Massachusetts Bottlers of the Merrimack Valley.

Without doubt, McQuade & Co. have the largest collecting agency in the city of Lowell, dealing only with responsible houses making quick returns for all business placed in their hands. He has associate collectors in every city of the United States, with whom he can correspond to reach any individual where the address is obtainable. He is also deputy collector for unpaid city taxes of the city of Lowell, has telephone connections, No. 351-4, and gives employment to five hands, two of whom are stenographers and three collectors, and he runs three teams.

Courtney & Courtney and Charles McIntire are the company's attorneys, and look after all legal matters. Mr. J. A. McQuade is a son of J. A. McQuade, deputy superintendent of police, who has held that position for the past few years. He is a native of Lowell and received his early education in the public schools. Mr. McQuade gives his personal attention to the details in the business and when a settlement is made the client receives his money within twenty-four hours thereafterwards.

FIFIELD TOOL COMPANY.

GEO. FIFIELD, PRESIDENT; E. W. THOMAS, VICE PRESIDENT;
JOHN J. DONOVAN, TREASURER.

DIRECTORS.

FRANCIS JEWETT, O. B. RANDLETT, GEO. T. SHELDON,
N. D. PRATT, G. H. MARSTON.

MOIR BROTHERS & CO.,

Merrimack St.

The enterprise of Moir Brothers & Co. was established in 1891 and has since built up a trade that places it in the front rank of its kind in Lowell. The premises occupied for the business comprise a front of about 30 feet and a depth of about 70 feet. The left-hand half of the store is devoted solely to a handsomely arranged millinery department

which is trimmed in the various seasons with all the modern "up-to-date" styles with prices in keeping with quality. Their line also embraces fancy goods, hose, underwear, gloves, dress trimmings, small ware, laces, ribbons, corsets, cotton underwear, jewelry, wrappers, yarns and fancy goods; while the store is largely devoted to French millinery, the rest of the goods are in harmony with the style; about 30 ladies are in attendance in the busy season, several being efficient masters of the French language.

F. U. CAMBRIDGE,

Pictures, Stationery and Periodicals. Merrimack House Block.

One of the oldest picture-frame, stationery and periodical houses in Lowell is that of F. U. Cambridge, located in the Merrimack House building, which was established by Cambridge Brothers, O. L. and F. U. Cambridge in 1873. Mr. Cambridge is a native of Lowell. The stock carried embraces every description of pictures, stationery and periodicals which are offered to the trade at reasonable prices.

The picture-frame works are located at the rear of the store, the dimensions of which are 120 x 40 feet. During the last five years the business has been personally managed by Mr. F. U. Cambridge. The energy and enterprise exhibited in the conduct of this house from its inception has resulted in an immense growth and substantial success.

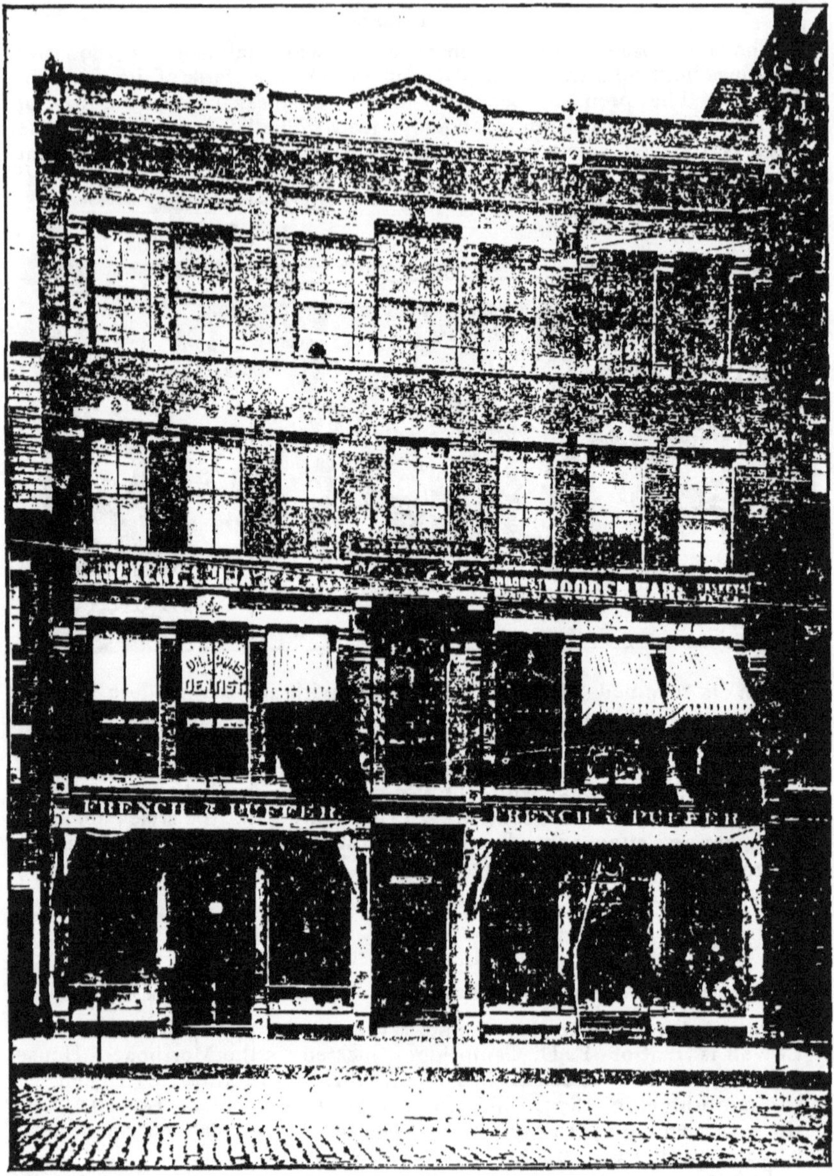
WOODEN WARE
DENTIST
FRENCH & PUFFER
FRENCH & PUFFER

FRENCH & PUFFER.,

Centarl St.

This firm is one of the oldest established in our city, and its progressive methods are recognized not only in our own city but through all New England where its offices and representatives are well known.

The founder ot this establishment, Mr. Amos B. French, died a few years since and his methods and work have been so exemplified that the business of the concern has greatly enlarged and was never so flourishing as it is today under the management of Mr. Freeman W. B. Puffer and Mr. Amos B. Leighton, the latter dating his connection with the firm since the death of Mr. French. French & Puffer are large importers of crockery, glass and china ware, and are wholesale dealers in wooden, tin and agate ware, and all their goods have the quality of being carefully selected under the supervision of a member of the firm.

For the next year the firm have in mind a series of elegant goods which they are to offer as catch bargains to be offered at cost prices. Probably no concern ot a similar character in the city has a more varied assortment in their line of goods than this firm, in buying large quantities, paying cash for all they get, and giving customers the benefit of advantages they themselves receive.

DR. F. L. FARRINGTON,

Dentist, 407 Middlesex St.

One of the leading dentists in Lowell is F. L. Farrington, whose place is located at 407 Middlesex St., where he has the most improved style of dental parlors, being handsomely carpeted, with two of the latest style chairs and cases, and one of the lightest rooms in the city, conducting all of his operations in the bay window. He also has a divided department where he conducts the manufacture of plate crowns, bridges, fillings, etc. It is near the Northern depot, and in a rapidly growing section of the city.

Mr. Farrington was born in Maine, and commenced the study of dentistry in 1876 with Dr. Clifford of Lowell; he also practiced in Boston in 1880, until 1882. Attended a course in dental surgery at New York college of Dentistry, returning to Lowell in 1885, at which time he was employed by a leading dentist, later taking his quarters at his present stand where he has built up an immense practice. No dentist in Lowell is better known than Dr. Farrington. His work is reliable, his prices are right and all work is guaranteed.

BUCKLAND & PATTERSON,

Printers.

The above firm does printing of all kinds at lowest possible rates. Both members of the firm are young and progressive men and practical printers. Their work is first-class in every particular. Their establishment is located at 74 Middle St.

One of Lowell's Largest Industries. Hood's Sarsaparilla.

COLUMBIA CASH REGISTER.

One of the important factors of Lowell's industries is the manufacture of cash registers. The Columbia is said to possess more good points than any register made, and it is only a matter of a very short time when its superiority over other makes will be recognized by the public.

The quarters on Middle St. are commodious and convenient, the floorage being 100 x 120 feet, and are now being fitted up with the most modern machinery especially adapted to their line of work. The officers are: Charles Tappan, president: William W. French, treasurer; and C. S. Trask, superintendent; the company was organized Sept. 18, 1894, since which time its growth has been phenomenal.

The company employs about 30 men and this number will be increased from time to time as the demand for increased product shall warrant. In connection with the register business, a nickel plating works is conducted, utilizing 6 to 8 vats constantly. The building where the plant is located is provided with both passenger and freight elevators and in fact, the company enjoys every possible facility for expeditiously filling all its orders. Workmanship and prices will be satisfactory.

JACQUES SHUTTLE CO.

The J. S. Jacques Shuttle Company ranks with the most famous representatives of the important industry in this country. The enterprise

had its conception in 1830 when J. S. Jacques began on a modest scale to manufacture shuttles, bobbins and spools, and among their construction of machinery can be found today the latest improved "up-to-date" style; and it may be fairly pronounced the founder of that line of industry. The premises of the company have been enlarged from time to time, and are situated in the United States Bunting yard, occupying a two-story brick building with a floorage of about 100 x 70 feet, and employing from 25 to 30 skilled workmen. They also have the use of two large storage buildings, 125 x 50 feet, which are directly opposite the factory. With thegrowth of the trade the facilities for manufacturing have been steadily augmented, until now it is among the largest of its kind in the city. Most of the product is sold in the New England states and a large amount goes to the West, South and Canada. The wide success this house has attained has been the result of conservative, practical, business management.

Mr. Jacques is a very old man and has seen the development of the city from childhood. He is also closely identified with other commercial interests as well as this industry.

ANNEX TO THE ROCKINGHAM.,

234 Central St.

A modern and most complete cafe and grill room on a par with any in the metropolitan city is now completed at 234 Central St., and will be connected with the present Rockingham Cafe. No expense will be spared to furnish the people of Lowell with an "up-to-date" restaurant that will exceed any in the city at the present time, and an assurance is

made by the proprietors of the Rockingham that the new department is to be conducted on the highest scale and in accordance with the desires of diners-out.

The location of the new cafe is one of the most accessible in the city, situated on Central St. For some time past the building in which the cafe is located, has been idle with the exception of the store in which the Rockingham bar is located The proprietors realizing that a first-class grill room and cafe is needed in the city decided to take the adjoining store and provide for the want of the ever increasing good livers of Lowell. In point of furnishing convenient services and a superior bar, the new cafe will far outstrip any previous attempt of its kind ever started in Lowell, and it is hoped by the proprietors of the Rockingham that their idea will meet with the approval of the people who appreciate a first-class place of this kind.

W. H. BROWN,

Cor. Appleton and Gorham Sts.

The well-known grocery house of W. H. Brown needs no comment as to location, for it is one of the most central, being directly opposite Lowell's new postoffice, giving Mr. Brown one of the best situations in this city. His stock embraces everything which one would expect in a first-class grocery store, both imported and domestic; canned goods, bottled goods, cheese, butter, eggs, teas, coffees, spices, pickles, flour, etc. Mr. Brown, personally, is constantly in attendance at his business and satisfaction in every department has been the result. He is a man who is interested in the growth and welfare of Lowell's industries, and is one of its leading grocers. Mr. Brown's practical business experience in connection with his proficient management has given the trade prices which are at all times in harmony with quality of goods.

He maintains a most rapid delivery system in which the most modern methods are used and all relations with this house will prove the above statements.

MISS A. W. BROWN.,

84 Middlesex St., Odd Fellows' Block. Moles Permanently Removed.

There is one successful method of permanently removing superfluous hair, moles and every facial blemish which is a constant source of annoyance to those who are afflicted with it. They are permanently removed by the electric needle, which is recommended by all reputable physicians. Ladies who are affected with this masculine deformity should not neglect it. There is no excuse for any lady to allow a growth of hair to remain upon her face which mars her personal beauty, and annoys her friends. All personal communications to Miss A. W. Brown will be gladly answered. Miss Brown's peculiar branch of surgery has been recently removed to larger and more pleasant quarters in room 7, Odd Fellows' building, Middlesex St., where she may be consulted between the hours of 9 and 12 and 2 to 4 p. m. daily, except Sunday. She has the reputation of being competent in removal of all facial blemishes without the slightest injury by its use. She has nicely located quarters at the above place and has a large patronage in her line.

M. STEINERT & SONS, CO.,

New England representatives for the Steinway & Sons, Hardman, Gabler, Standard and Bacon Pianofortes. 1863-Thirty Years-1895.

Steinert Hall, 190 Tremont St. Boston. This company's great variety of makes and immense stock of several hundred pianos furnish the most favorable circumstances under which the puzzling piano problem can possibly be solved, as thousands of their customers will testify. They are also sole representatives of the wonderful self-playing Aeolian. This marvellous instrument renders all kinds of music in a manner pleasing to the most critical, and can be readily mastered by any member of the family. Its great popularity with orchestral conductors is ample proof of its merits. It must be seen and heard to be fully appreciated.

The public are cordially invited to call at their Lowell warerooms, 51 Merrimack St, before purchasing any instrument. Other branches: New Haven, Providence, Portland, Worcester, Newport, Springfield, Philadelphia, Lawrence andBridgeport.

M. Steinert & Sons, Co., leading pianoforte dealers in New England.

GUMB BROTHERS.

Monuments.

These well-known marble cutters, designers, manufacturers and importers of fine marble and granite monuments are, without a doubt, the leading men in their line in the city of Lowell. The business was established in 1885 by Willam Andrews and is located near the Edson cemetery at 1258 Gorham St. Messrs. R. G. and H. M. Gumb are natives of Nova Scotia, but have been residents of Lowell for the past sixteen years. Their marble yard covers an area of 18,000 feet of land with sheds under which many skilled workmen accomplish their work, under the personal supervision of the brothers, who are both practical designers of memorial stone monuments. The office and salesroom is located on Gorham St., directly in the front of the yard where are displayed finished goods, with a full line of pretty designs so that no one need be turned away for lack of proficient and artistic work. Their prices are always in harmony with first class workmanship and quality of goods. They make a specialty of inscribing monuments, resetting bases, removing the same, etc.

The practical experience of Gumb Brothers is one point of interest to be looked upon, which but few marble establishments can speak of, as it enables one to attend to the designing department, while the other oversees the general work. This house has grown so in the past few years that it stands prominent among the establishments of its kind in the city. No doubt honorable and strict methods is the key to their past success.

ELECTRICITY.

The artificial illumination of Lowell, aside from the gas, and gasoline lights—the latter in the suburbs only— rests entirely with one large and flourishing body, the Lowell Electric Light Corporation. Ii is a body which first organized on a small scale and gradually extended its scope so as to entirely control the business of lighting our streets, places of business and even homes, with electricity. The corpòration is purely of local origin and Lowell men still control and guide its fortunes. It was first organized in 1881 under state laws, with a capital of $10,000, commencing with two Weston arc light machines, leasing power from an accommodating saw mill. A year later, the Middlesex Electric Light Company was formed and established a small plant on Middle street. The Thomson-Houston system was introduced, and a little later the lattér company bought out the Weston Company. The business increased as the demand for electric lighting became general, and the Middle St. plant became one of no mean·proportions. Seven years ago, the company reorganized under the name it now bears; steps were taken to secure a site for a plant which would fully meet future requirments, which was secured on the line of the Boston & Maine Railroad, in Belvidere, and operations commenced.

The officers of the company are: George W. Fifield, president; William A. Ingham, vice-president; John H. McAlvin, treasurer and secretary; L. I. Fletcher, manager; directors, G. W. Fifield, W. A. Ingham, J. H. McAlvin, L. I. Fletcher, Lowell; James H. Tolles, Charles F. Collins, Nashua, N. H.; Cyrus Conant, Concord, Mass.

F. A. TUTTLE,

This leading and important retail house was established by Mr. F. A. Tuttle, and has since proved a prominent factor in the retail grocery and provision business. He has a fine site located at 329 and 331 Thorndike street, facing Davis Square. The premises occupied for the business comprise a commodious double store of about 100 square feet, one store being used exclusively for meats and provisions, the other for groceries and fruits. He employs six hands, runs three delivery wagons, and has telephone connections.

They make a specialty of country produce, etc. Their fine facilities for delivery places this house in the front ranks of its line. Mr. Tuttle gives the business his personal attention and his assistants are all polite and courteous. Mr. Tuttle is a progressive and substantial business man of Lowell.

EARLE BRYANT,

Carriage Manufacturer, West Third St.

The enterprise ot E. P. Bryant was established in 1884 and he has since built up a trade that places it in the front ranks of its line in Lowell. This house deals strictly in first class workmanship and its trade extends throughout the surrounding counties and is annually increasing. The premises occupied for the business are large and commodious and comprise two floors, with a floorage of 110 x 35 feet on each floor. Up stairs is the painting department and on the ground floor is the repair shop, in rear of which is the manufacturing department. Mr. Bryant gives his personal supervision to the business and employs fifteen hands. The house sustains the highest reputation for fair and honorable dealings.

FREDERIC LEEDS,

Railway & Steamship Agency.

We are all like Coxey and would like to obtain our railroad and steamship tickets for nothing, or if not for nothing, as cheap as we can. Acting on the supposition that the people of Lowell were not different from the majority, Mr. Frederic B. Leeds opened an office at 15 Central St., for the sale of all kinds of tickets at less than tarift rates.

It was amusing to notice the fears of some timid "would-be" customers who wished to get their tickets, and so save several dollars, but their minds were filled with the stories spread broadcast about scalpers' tickets being taken away from them on the train and having to pay fare. But when it was explained that Mr. Leeds belonged to the American Ticket Brokers' Association, a society having members in all parts of the country, and that he would guarantee every ticket was just as he represented, they took advantage of the greatly reduced rates he could give on the first-class routes, and now it has come to be the custom for people going to travel to trade with Leeds at 15 Central St.

CHAS. LESLIE SWEETSIR, M. D.,

He was born in Saco, Maine, in 1869, and received his early education in the Saco public schools, then after four years of study graduated from Thornton Academy.

He began the study of medicine with Dr. F. E. Maxcy of Saco, now of Washington. D. C., one year before entering Medical College. Graduated from the Portland Medical School and the Maine Medical School, receiving the best of hospital advantages in both. He was associated one year with Dr. S. F. Weeks of Portland in his office. Dr Weeks is professor of surgery in the Medical School and has a reputation as a surgeon second to none in the country. Was also associated one year with Dr. Seth C. Gordon of Portland, specialist in diseases of women. The following year he was resident physician at the Lowell General Hospital, since which time he has been practicing in Lowell with excellent success.

FAY BROS. & HOSFORD,

Carriage Repository Central St.

The important enterprise of Fay Bros. & Hosford was established by Edgar L. and Orbert Fay in the year of 1881, and in 1883 A. H. Hosford (son of Hon. ex-Mayor Hosford, of this city) identified himself with it under the firm name of Fay Bros & Hosford. The building on Central street with its five stories has a floorage of about one quarter of an acre. This firm has also a large three story house on Elm street. In their establishment on Central street is conducted the sale of pleasure vehicles and business wagons, repair department and trimming.

Messrs. Fay Bros. & Hosford are also proprietors of the Lowell Opera House (a picture of which will be found elsewhere in this book) which is said to be second to none outside of Boston, in the New England states.

SCANNELL & WHOLEY.

Scannell & Wholey's boiler shop is the largest of its kind in Lowell; employs from 50 to 75 men and occupies a roomy and commodious building on Tanner street. It has close accommodations with the Boston & Maine Railroad, which gives it the advantage of receiving and shipping goods to all parts of the United States.

The members of the firm are practical manufacturers and enterprising business men. The accompanying cut is a picture of its works and bears the established date of 1880.

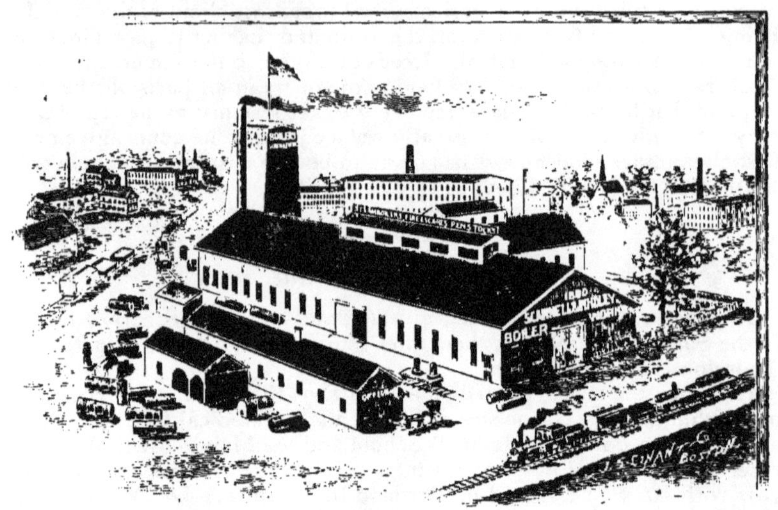

Mr. Scannell has the honor of being local boiler inspector, and no doubt is the best authority in this district in his line of business. Both Mr. Scannell and Mr. Wholey give the business their personal attention in all departments. This concern may justly be awarded great credit for supplying the demands of the trade in their line. Their workmanship is not only first class, but prices are always in harmony with quality of same.

LOWELL WALL PAPER CO,

Ingham's Block, Church St.

The enterprise now conducted by Mr. Chase in Ingham's Block, where he has the finest quarters in the city of Lowell to carry on the wall paper and window shade business, has grown to be a large establishment.

This house is in direct touch with the manufacturers and designers of all grades of wall paper, and Mr. Chase is in a position to give the public better advantages than any other house in the city of Lowell. His quarters in the Ingham Block are finely situated in the second story, where his shelves hold some of the most elegant designs and imitation of fresco walls that have ever been exhibited. This firm has the reputation of carrying the highest artistic talent in its accomplishment, making a specialty of interior decoration of private houses, clubs, cafes, theatres, public buildings and apartments, from original designs, producing the richest and most pleasing effects. The firm has executed work of this character in many of the finest buildings in the city of Lowell and vicinity, where they have had an opportunity to fully demonstrate their skill and ability.

The establishment is a most important factor of the trade resources of Lowell and its honorable record of a full quarter of a century is the best possible evidence of its vigorous and popular industry. Mr. Chase is a broad guage, progressive business man under whose personal observation the business is conducted.

J. B. COVER & Co.,

29, 31 and 33 Shattuck St., Hay, Grain. Flour and Feed.

One of the most prominent enterprises of the kind in the city of Lowell is the establishment of J. B. Cover & Co., which is located at 29, 31 and 33 Shattuck street. Mr. Cover was established in business about twenty years ago, at which time he began in a single store at No. 33 Shattuck street. A part of that time Mr. Cover was associated with a friend and with a brother. In 1894, Mr. O. J. Davis, who was associated with Boutwell Bros. for nearly fifteen years, became identified with the concern. Boutwell Bros. at that time were located in the identical spot at 29 Shattuck street where a part of J. B. Cover & Co.'s establishment is at present. They took this store at 29 Shattuck street in order to facilitate their business, and today it is safe to say they rank among the leading concerns in their line, which has been attained only by strict policy and fair square dealings. Their premises for storage and reserve stock at the three above numbers have dimensions of 90 x 100 feet, making a very spacious building for their business, which embraces hay, straw, oats, corn, meal, wheat, shorts, flour, oat meals, fertilizer, etc.

PIPER & MACDONALD,

160 Lincoln St.

Few people have any conception of the enormous business which has grown up within the past few years at 160 Lincoln street, at the establishment of Piper & MacDonald, who are retail and wholesale dealers in groceries, provisions, meats, vegetables, canned goods, crockery, etc. This house was established in 1893, and has ever since increased its trade till now it extends throughout the section of Ayer City. The premises occupied by Messrs. Piper & MacDonald are very spacious, covering about 25,000 square feet of land, directly opposite Haworth & Watson's conical cope tube works.

The goods are procured direct from the original sources of supply and the advantages and inducements offered to buyers are such as appertain only to a house that is conducted upon the most approved methods, enjoying unsurpassed facilities in delivery of goods and conducted under experienced and progressive business men. This house will be found equal to all the requirements of customers in its line, and operations are conducted upon the most liberal and fair dealing methods.

MERRIMACK TEA CO.,

Corner Worthen and Market Sts.

One of the liveliest and long established houses in Lowell, engaged in handling teas, coffees, crockery, glass ware, etc., is the retail house of the Merrimack Tea Company. This progressive house was founded in 1894 by its present manager, Mr. Daniel Desmond, and in the course of a year and a half has proved its usefulness in the industrial line of this city. The lines of this concern embrace Young Hyson, English Breakfast, Japan, Black Tea, making a specialty of Oolong.

In catering to the demands of the trade in this community, this house offers advantages of quick delivery, and prices are in harmony with quality.

The active manager is Daniel Desmond, who is a progressive and substantial business man, and is interested in the progress of Lowell. The Merrimack Tea Company has gained its fame by selling reliable goods at moderate prices, with honorable dealings, correct weight, exchange of tickets for crockery, prompt delivery and looking closely after the interests of their customers in every legitimate manner, at the same time developing a business that is creditable to our community.

JAMES H. SPARKS, VETERINARY SURGEON,

Livery, Baiting, Boarding and Hack Stables, 154 Worthen St.

No close observer in the city can find a more accommodating livery, baiting and sales stable than that of James H. Sparks. It is most centrally situated, having accommodations for about 80 horses and controling 25 vehicles of every description. It has the largest floor space of any in the city, possibly larger than some in the metropolis. It has a floorage of about three-quarters of an acre; it has the personal supervision of a veterinary surgeon; it has accommodating attaches; it has all the modern improvements, such as wash stands, light stables, concrete ground floor with plenty of storage room, and every convenience which goes to make up a modern livery, boarding and sales stable.

Mr. Sparks' establishment is certainly a large factor in Lowell's progress. There is no house of its kind in the city which rents finer hacks, coupes, barouches and general livery.

The high standing and responsibility of this house is widely known and its success is attributed to its liberal dealings, reasonable prices and satisfactory accommodations to the trade.

F. M. BILL,

Wholesale Grocer, Produce Merchant, 98 to 102 Middle St.

Within recent years great progress has been made in the wholesale grocery and produce trade. Among one of the most favored is the house of F. M. Bill, which was originally instituted in 1890 at 81 Middle street. In 1892 he removed to more commodious premises at the above numbers. The supremacy this house has for the past five years fulfilled in an exceptional manner in providing the grocery and produce consumers with the most reliable goods in the country, which has been the result of the adoption of new and advanced methods and the exercise of enterprise and energy on the part of its proprietor.

The premises now occupied for the business are centrally located and finely appointed, consisting of a four story brick structure with a ground floor and basement, each having a floorage of 100 x 60 feet, with sub-verandas for reserved stock. Mr. Bill handles many special products which are not obtainable elsewhere in this market, among which may be noted the agency for Erie Preserved Canned Goods Co. of Buffalo, which has become famous. Mr. Bill gives employment to about ten hands, two of whom are travelling salesmen on the road, five inside and three teamsters. They also enjoy a promptness in unloading freight directly at the rear of the store, where two carloads can be relieved of their contents at a time, enabling them to make transactions in trade with prompt delivery and satisfaction.

DUMAS' BOOK BINDING ESTABLISHMENT,

Ingham's Block, Church St.

Lowell is entitled to the credit of being able to support a large and creditable bookbinding establishment, which is the noted one of Dumas & Co., located in the Ingham Block on Church street. The premises occupied for headquarters of the business are composed of a handsome five story and basement building, which is known as the Ingham Building, a sketch of which will be found elsewhere.

The high standing and responsibility of the firm are widely known, resulting from ample supplies to meet the requirements of the trade. The manager, Mr. Dumas, is not a figurehead but a practical, long experienced book binder who understands the business in every detail. He also accomplished the binding of this book.

GEORGE HARLIN PILLSBURY, M. D.

George Harlin Pillsbury, son of Dr. Harlin and Sophia Bigelow (Pratt) Pillsbury, was born in Lowell, June 8th, 1843. He attended the Lowell High School and Dartmouth College, receiving his degree of A. B. from Dartmouth in the class of 1866. He was graduated from Harvard Medical School in 1869. Immediately after his graduation he went to Europe, where he remained one year, most of the time in the hospitals in Paris. He entered upon the practice of his profession in Lowell, in June 1870, where he now remains.

He has served on the staff of St. John's Hospital since 1873, and was president of the Middlesex North District Society in 1878 and 1879.

Dr. Pillsbury is a thoroughly educated man, a good writer and a finished speaker. He has devoted his life nevertheless to the assiduous duties of a hardworking family physician, with a large practice, and is today perhaps the best representative of the general practitioners of the city.

A. F. STORY & CO.,

Druggists.

Among the early established and important representative enterprises of Davis' Square is the well-known drug store of A. F. Story & Co., which was originally established in 1856, and has changed hands but few times until 1891, when it came into the possession of A. F. Story & Co. The location is 337 Thorndike St., Davis Square. It occupies the most prominent spot with a frontage of about 30 feet and a depth of about 90. The interior of this drug store is well equipped. Among the many noted fixtures is that of a fine soda fountain, and it has been said that no store in Lowell draws a more refreshing glass of soda than is drawn from this counter.

He has milk shake machines, ice cream chests, ice shavers and fancy syrup cylinders, finely appointed cigar cases, and confectionery cases just above.

The general appearance of this drug store is in keeping with its management, whose principles and methods are "up-to-date."

The Flaxseed Compound manufactured by Story, for coughs and colds has become famous, the demand for which is very large.

G. FORREST MARTIN, M. D.

Dr. Martin is one of Lowell's younger physicians who is rapidly pushing forward into the front ranks of his profession. He is an Ohioan by birth, having been born in Mason, Warren Co., Ohio in 1862, but the greater part of his life has been spent in Lowell, where he is well known, and where his early education was obtained. After graduating from the Lowell High School in 1879, Dr. Martin took a course in Bryant & Stratton's Business College, Boston. In 1886 he commenced reading medicine in the office of that veteran homoeopathic practician, Dr. H. Hunter, and then went to New York City for study. He attended three courses of lectures at the New York Homoeopathic Medical College and hospital, and at graduation took the first faculty prize for scholarship. Anxious to get immediately to work, Dr. Martin bought out a well established practice in central New York, where he remained for four years in active, general work.

In October, 1893, he sold his practice and removed to Lowell. Dr. Martin is one who is heartily in love with his work. While in college, instead of taking the customary five months, summer vacation, he spent that time in the hospital and clinics of New York and Brooklyn, obtaining that practical knowledge which they so well afford. Since coming to Lowell, he has spent much time in Boston hospitals and clinics, paying special attention to general surgery and diseases of women.

While attending to a rapidly increasing general practice, Dr. Martin will continue to pay particular attention to the above special branches. In general practice he is an ardent, but liberal minded homoeopath. He is a member of the staff of the Homoeopathic Free Dispensary and of the Lowell General Hospital, and is the attending physician to the Ayer Home for Young Women and Children. Dr. Martin is married, has one daughter, and resides at 70 Fourth St. His office is at 17 Kirk St.

GOLDEN SHEAF & ROCHESTER,

Middle St.

At the head of Lowell's wholesale and retail liquor trade stands the newly established and prominent house of J. M. Pevey, which was founded about a year and a half ago in the wholesale business only, but who about three months ago opened a retail department in connection with the Golden Sheaf, which is called the Rochester.

The interior of both the Rochester and Golden Sheaf are the brightest of any cafe in the city of Lowell. Headquarters of the house are embraced in a spacious warehouse, having about 60 feet front with large plate glass. The place is open for inspection and the highest class of trade is carried on. On the right of the retail department is a number of well situated stalls. The partition between the wholesale and retail departments divides them in the front upon entering, and a cash desk directly at the left of the bar is looked after by a young lady in the wholesale department.

Mr. Pevey occupies a handsome office and the liquors in the glass cases are displayed with great taste. The interior is all white, with gold trimmings, and adorned with mirrors in every section. Mr. Pevey has met with the greatest success and with the wholesale trade has fully held his own. The business is conducted under Mr. Pevey's personal attention, both in the retail and wholesale department. He gives employment to about eight hands. Wholesale goods are promptly delivered and fair dealings have made this progressive enterprise a success.

F. W. CHENEY & CO.

The leading hardware concern of Davis Square is that of F. W. Cheney & Co., and is larger in some respects than some of the more central hardware houses. This house was established in 1889. The business is personally managed by F. W. Cheney and J. A. Thompson, both of whom are natives of Lowell.

Mr. F. W. Cheney, the purchaser, brings great practical knowledge on every detail of the hardware trade, as well as the requirements of customers. The premises occupied by them are located at 5 and 6 Davis Square and are composed of a handsome double front store of about 70 x 100 with adjoining department for storage. The stock carried embraces every imaginable article of use in the hardware line, such as farming utensils, garden hose, mill supplies, paints, oils, brushes, ice cream freezers, flour seeds, hammocks, etc.

A. H. STANLEY,

Trunk Manufacturer.

Mr. A. H. Stanley began the trunk business at the age of 13 years in this city, having served his juniorship. He took the position of foreman of the largest trunk manufactory in the city of Boston and held that position for eight years, at the expiration of which time he located in Lowell, and about a year ago he established a factory at No. 48 and 50 Middlesex street.

The premises occupied for the manufacture of trunks are the most ample of any house in the city of Lowell, having a floor space of about 150 x 40, salesroom and trunk department.

Mr. Stanley is a skilled workman in his line, having had about 29 years experience in making trunks, valises, harness, etc., and the stock shown at his place is always modern and complete. He not only makes trunks, bags and harness paraphernalia but includes the novelties of small leather goods such as satchels, pocketbooks, music cases, etc.

He is a progressive business man and it is safe to predict his success will be unlimited in the future, for the conservative management under which the business is conducted assures success to all his departments. It is a house especially to be relied upon in representation of goods, prices being always in harmony with quality.

R. HARMSTON.

New and second hand furniture are articles of daily utility, and it is well to become posted as to where the place is located, what the stock consists of, and who the members of the firm are, etc. Mr. Harmston is a man of wide experience in the furniture business, having learned the trade over twenty years ago. After filling a position in one of Lowell's leading furniture houses for five years, he started a small second hand store on Market street; finding his business increasing so rapidly, he removed to 173 Middlesex street, where he found a more spacious location. He at once stocked up with a new and large line of second hand goods, such as chamber sets, parlor sets and everything of like nature; he has also the Harmston ranges and parlor heaters. On these goods the prices are all right; it has also been said that no man in this city is more capable of finishing and polishing a piano than Mr. Harmston.

He employs at present four skilled hands who conduct the upholstering department, where hair mattresses are repaired or made to order; in fact this house sells everything, buys everything or exchanges anything from a piano stool to a farm; they also repair stoves, and carry on a general selling, buying and trading business. If anyone has anything to sell, just drop them a line and they will call on you and do business with you; satisfaction guaranteed in every respect.

PARKER & BASSETT,

Manufacturers of Manilla Paper.

This well-known house has greatly added to Lowell's large list of manufactures and has made for itself a reputation such as can only be founded upon first-class goods and standard workmanship. The firm has large, accommodating premises located at Dracut. The factory is equipped with the most modern machinery and the business is managed by progressive business men of high standing who are both honorable as well as conservative.

Their trade extends generally throughout the New England states; they have an ample force of salesmen who call on the trade; they also manufacture for large jobbing houses in the principal cities of this country.

A. L, BROOKS & CO.,

Mechanics Mills, Dutton & Fletcher Sts.

Among the representative establishments engaged in the lumber business in Lowell, special mention may be made of this house, which was founded by Mr. A. L. Brooks in 1835. It was the first concern in Lowell to do wood work by machinery. The late Thomas P. Goodhue was his partner at that time, having had experience in connection with Mr. Brooks, and under whose direction the business was managed.

A few years later Mr. William Fisk succeeded Mr. Goodhue, at which time the business was conducted in the Middlesex corporation building. In 1845 they removed to their present quarters, a building which covers over three quarters of an acre in floor space and is occupied by the following concerns: J. C. Carter & Co., wood turning and cut work; A. J. Alley, who is widely known as the leading pattern maker of Lowell; J. Tripp & Co., roll manufacturers; William Kelley, sash, blind and door manufacturer; John Welch, furniture manufacturer; M. C. Dupont, interior house materials; M. Aldrich, manufacturer of wooden screws and the Caruthers reeds and loom harness, and Hibbert & Smith, blind factory.

The Mechanics Mills were first operated by A. L. Brooks & Co., who were the first to introduce machinery in wood work in this city, and they have been a growing factor in this branch of trade for over a quarter of a century. They have good facilities for receiving and shipping, the depot being very nearly opposite the mills, receiving their materials direct from the original sources, and logs and trees via the Merrimack river from New Hampshire.

The factory and yard being located adjacent to the railroad afford it facilities that are superior for the prompt fulfilment of orders and shipment. It is creditable to the concern and patrons of this reputable house that they rank among the enterprising business men and members of prosperous manufacturing establishments.

WHEELER & WILSON,

Sewing Machine, Lowell Salesroom 360 Merrimack St.

One of the oldest enterprises in the city is the Wheeler & Wilson Machine Co. which has salesrooms at the above location. The factory of this most famous machine is situated in the city of Bridgeport, Conn., and is without doubt the largest machine manufactory in the United States. The salesroom is a pleasant one, being directly opposite the City Hall, with a frontage of about 30 feet and a depth of 125, in which is on exhibition a number of their later improvements in machines, in all styles, coloring and designs of cases. In the rear is a well adapted establishment where repairs are made. All attachments of the Wheeler & Wilson machine can be procured there.

The Lawrence corporation and Beaver Knitting company use a number of the Wheeler & Wilson machines, and for the past three years, since Mr. William Waterman has had charge of the Lowell business, it has met with great success. He is a practical business man and identified with the industrial advancement of Lowell.

DR. WILLIAM BASS.

William Bass, son of Joel, Jr., and Catherine Wright (Burnham) Bass, was born in Williamstown, Vt., June 22, 1832. He received his degree of M. D. in 1856, and came at once to Lowell, associating himself in practice with Dr. Walter Burnham.

In 1858 he left Lowell for the West, but at the end of two years he returned. He served as assistant surgeon in the Sixth Regiment Massachusetts Volunteers for several months in 1864.

Dr. Bass is a general practitioner, although he has given much attention to surgery. He has always been a constant attendant at the meetings of the Middlesex North District Medical Society, and has been elected to nearly every office in the gift of the society, being president in 1884 and 1885. He has been on the staff of the Corporation hospital and is at present on the surgical staff of St. John's hospital. He has been physician to the Old Ladies' Home from the establishment of that institution. He married, Oct. 5, 1856, Elizabeth Gates Hunt.

DRESSMAKERS' LEAGUE,

Associate Building.

The Dressmakers' League was established about three year ago and has ever since enjoyed an unbroken career of growth and progression, ranking today with the most famous dressmaking establishments in this section of the country. It is under an experienced and enterprising conductor but the facilities have proved inefficient to meet the abnormal growth of the immense trade and they have enlarged their place giving three large rooms to the enterprise. They make a specialty of ladies' wraps, ladies' jackets, robes, capes, garments, underwear and everything in women's wearing apparel. The prices are always in harmony with the good workmanship and quality of goods, and it has been said that the prices are much lower in many instances than in any other establishment of its kind in the city of Lowell. The point of this house is to excel and they have done their full share in the development of the dressmaking industry of this city. It is one of the coming industries of the city of Lowell and success and prosperity will surely be the outcome. If you look elsewhere you will find a cut of building.

JOHN CARROLL IRISH, A. B., M. D.

John Carroll Irish, son of Cyrus and Catharine (Davis) Irish, was born at Buckfield, Me , Sept. 30, 1843. He received his degree of A. B. at Dartmouth in the class of 1868, and his medical degree at the Bellevue Hospital Medical College in 1872. He commenced practice in Buckfield, remaining there until November, 1874, when he came to Lowell. While in Maine he was a member of the Board of Examining Surgeons of Pensions. He has been in Lowell since 1874, and has practiced surgery almost exclusively, giving special attention to ovariotomy. Up to this date he has made over a hundred abdominal operations, principally ovariotomies and hysterectomies.

He has read and published papers as follows: "Reasons for the early removal of Ovarian Tumors," "A discussion of the statistics of Ovariotomy," "Two and one half years' experience in Abdominal Surgery," "Laparotomy for Pus in the Abdominal Cavity and for Peritonitis," "Treatment of Uterine Myo-Fibromata by Abdominal Hysterectomy." He was appointed medical examiner for this district in 1877 by Governor Rice, and at the expiration of his term of seven years, in 1884 was reappointed by Governor Robinson, and, by virtue of that appointment, is still in office.

MURPHY & BINGHAM,

Boarding, Livery and Hack Stables, 380 to 386 Middlesex St.

A leading and beneficial factor in the city of Lowell is the boarding, livery and hack stable of Murphy & Bingham, which was established in 1888. Messrs. Murphy & Bingham succeeded C. F. Keyes, and Mr. Keyes succeeded Mr. Huntoon, but it has never done so prosperous a business as under the present management of Messrs. Murphy and Bingham. Mr. Murphy is a native of Lowell and Mr. Bingham is a native of Vermont. They feed and board about 40 horses which are stalled and groomed on the second floor.

The building occupied for the purpose is one of the largest in Lowell, having three floors about 125 x 75 feet, the third floor being used for storage, the second for horses and the first, which is asphalt paved, for hacks, carriages, etc. This favorite establishment is open all night and has telephone connection, the number of which is 1084. They run hacks and general livery. They also have connected with the stable the well known veterinary surgeon, A. H. McCann, who is a graduate of Toronto Veterinary College. They are the owners of a wagon called the six passenger wagon and a wagonette for special purposes.

They employ about twelve hands in the stable and the business is conducted under the personal management of Messrs. Murphy and Bingham, both of whom are well known in Lowell and are a credit to the industrial forces of this city. This house has gained a reputation for providing excellent board for horses.

HORACE B. SHATTUCK,

Hardware and Bicycle Dealers, Central St.

Among the leading representatives of the hardware business in Lowell is the popular and influential firm of Shattuck & Son, who occupy handsome and well appointed stores on Central and Prescott streets. This firm began business in a very small way, Horace Shattuck being the founder, and in late years his son became identified with the business conducting the bicycle department on Prescott street. They represent only the leading bicycles which embrace every possible quality of improvement and have the very best reputation in the wheel line. The house of Horace B. Shattuck has developed very rapidly and has built for itself a reputation which has only been accomplished through fair dealings. It is closely identified with the commercial interest and advancement of the industrial welfare of the community.

SIMPSON & ROWLAND,

Wholesale Grocers, 82, 84 & 86 Middle St.

An old established and leading representative of the wholesale grocery and produce trade of Lowell is the house of Simpson & Rowland which was founded some 25 years ago by Mr. Simpson. About eight years ago he took in the partner of C. F. Rowland and it has since been one of the factors in the development of this trade in Lowell through its present magnitude.

The facilities of the house embrace commodious premises comprising four floors and cellar, which are well adapted to the requirements of the business, and the stock carried covers a general line of staple fancy goods in a great variety. The house enjoys intimate relations with shippers and producers and is in daily receipt of first consignments of every description. The Boston & Maine railroad runs a branch track directly in the rear of this large establishment, at which place two carloads can be unloaded at once.

Messrs. Simpson & Rowland are widely known to the trade as broad guage and progressive business men anxious to provide dealers with the most advanced accommodations. That their efforts are appreciated is evident by the growth and success of their business which is not exceeded in volume by that of any other house in its line. The business policy of the house is a reliable and fair dealing one and spirit of enterprise pervades all its efforts and places it in the front ranks of the commercial resources of Lowell. They also have a spice mill and coffee roasting department, which is located on the top floor.

Their trade extends throughout the surrounding territories, and there is no doubt that the above house is the largest outside of the metropolis in the New England states. The enterprise certainly contributes in no small degree to the general prosperity of this city and vicinity, and its high standing and reputation has won it the entire confidence of the trade.

TEMPLE OF DESIGN,

14 Merrimack St. Runels Bldg.

One of the well-known millinery establishments in Lowell is the Temple of Design which is located at the above number, of which A. M. Bird & Co. are proprietors. This is one of the most centrally located millinery establishments, being directly opposite the electric car waiting-room. The interior is nicely decorated with millinery goods of the most modern style, with handsome fixtures and attractively dressed windows.

It gives employment to about six people who are skilled in the millinery art. It is a growing establishment which has held its own, and its reputation is of the very best, standing in the front ranks of the millinery line. Their goods are always in harmony with prices and many advantages are obtainable that cannot be found elsewhere. No other millinery house is more liberal or more efficiently managed, and its success has been the result of fair dealings and well directed efforts.

INDEX.

www.ingramcontent.com/pod-product-compliance
Lightning Source LLC
Chambersburg PA
CBHW020547270326
41927CB00006B/748